HIKING & BIKING THE I&M CANAL

NATIONAL HERITAGE CORRIDOR

by Jim Hochgesang

Editing and Nature Notes by Sheryl DeVore
Design by Melanie Lawson

A Roots & Wings Publication

Dedication

A special thanks to the women and men involved in developing and maintaining the trails and pathways throughout Chicagoland and the I&M Canal National Heritage Corridor.

Created by Sandy and Jim Hochgesang.
Offset printing service by Rheitone, Inc.
Printed and bound by United Graphics, Inc.

Photography credits:
Front cover: Terry Farmer, Courtesy of the Illinois Department of Commerce and Community Affairs.
Back Cover:
Lock #6, Channahon, Courtesy Heritage Corridor Convention and Visitors Bureau
Prickly Pear Cactus by Hank Erdmann
White egrets, Courtesy Forest Preserve District of Will County

ISBN 1-884721-06-0

 Printed on recycled paper.

Contents

Acknowledgments

We appreciate the support, input, and guidance of many professionals who reviewed our draft manuscript, provided source maps, and supplied information.

Bill Banks, City of Palos Heights
Bill Weidner, Forest Preserve District of DuPage County
Bob Noonan, Heritage Corridor Convention and Visitors Bureau
Cathy Hudzik, Friends of the Chicago River
Debbie Greene, Joliet Park District
Ders Anderson, Openlands Project
Don Fisher, City of Joliet
George Bellovics, Jill Bergstrom, Jon Blume, Stacey Powers, and
	Chadd Safarcyk, Illinois Department of Natural Resources
John O'Lear, Forest Preserve District of Cook County
Lee Hanson & George Berndt, I&M Canal Commission
Lynn Kurczewski and Ralph Schultz, Forest Preserve District of
	Will County
Michelle Story, Lockport Township Park District
Reece Lukei, American Discovery Trail Society
Pat Thrasher, U. S. Forest Service
Steve Gulden, Romeoville Recreation Department
Steve Jones, Village of Lemont
Valerie Spale, Save the Prairie Society

Introduction

In 1984, Congress established the nation's first national heritage corridor to preserve the historic sites and natural areas along the 97-mile Illinois & Michigan (I&M) Canal. Running from the Chicago River at Bridgeport in Cook County to Peru in LaSalle County, the canal provided transport for barges, passenger packets, and later, recreation boats from 1848 to 1933. The creation of the I&M Canal National Heritage Corridor (NHC), recognized the national contribution made by the canal and preserved the remnants of the locks, bridges, and aqueducts that formed the main transportation route from the Great Lakes to the Mississippi River in the mid-19th century.

This guidebook focuses on two areas: first, the many off-road trails and bike paths that are part of the NHC, and second, all the trails in Will County, which was the center of activity during the construction of the canal 150 years ago. In so doing, this guidebook completes our Chicagoland series. Previous books describe the trails of Cook, DuPage, Lake, Kane, and McHenry Counties.

The NHC extends from Navy Pier in downtown Chicago to Lock #15 where the I&M Canal flows into the Illinois River at LaSalle/Peru.

Along the way, the NHC encompasses all or parts of 49 communities and parts of five counties (Cook, DuPage, Will, Grundy, and LaSalle). You will find many beautiful forest preserves, state parks, and other natural areas along the way. Some are directly adjacent to the canal. Others are nearby.

The NHC is a study in contrasts. The forests, prairies, canyons, ravines, rivers, and wetlands are interspersed at some spots with oil refineries, huge storage tanks, manufacturing facilities, and quarries. The canal provided a major transport route for raw materials and finished products. Chicago began evolving into the transportation center of the Midwest because of the canal and the industry that developed along the waterway.

As well as helping preserve the aqueducts, buildings, locks, and other relics of the historic canal, the NHC is filled with hiking and biking trails. The NHC trail system is a work in progress with many trails already in place, others under construction, and others still in the planning phase. Publication of this guidebook in 1998 is appropriate in that the Sesquicentennial anniversary of the I&M Canal's opening in 1848 is being celebrated from April 1998 to April 1999.

When in operation, the canal was a minimum of 60-feet wide and 6-feet deep. That is no longer true today. Development over the past 65 years since the canal was closed for boating, as well as natural sedimentation, has resulted in some areas where the waterway has vanished or nearly vanished from view. For example, the Stevenson Expressway (I-55) was built on a portion of the canal right-of-way. However, along most of the original 97-mile route, you can hike and bike on the original canal tow path at several trails (e.g. the 61-mile I&M Canal State Trail, Cook County's I&M Canal Bicycle Trail, and the Gaylord Donnelley Canal Trail in Lockport).

The canal right-of-way serves as a natural greenway where wetlands, prairies, and woodlands flourish. As we describe the hiking and biking trails, we will include information about some of the flora and fauna found in the natural areas surrounding the trails. We have also included a bit of history of the NHC starting on page 13. This is merely a sampling to give you an overview and to whet your appetite. History buffs will enjoy the many NHC visitor centers and interpretive trails. There is no better way to see the natural areas, communities and historic sights along the I&M Canal than on bike or on foot.

The second major focus of this guidebook is to provide a comprehensive guide of Will County trails. The field headquarters for the construction of the I&M Canal were located in Will County at Lockport. Today Will County is one of the fastest growing areas in Chicagoland with many new home developments springing up throughout the county on what were once corn fields. The Forest Preserve District of Will County (FPDWC) is working to preserve and restore open lands while recognizing and responding to the growing interest in off-road trails and bike paths. Several new trails have recently been completed. More are planned. We will describe all these trails in this guidebook.

How to Use This Guide:

On pages 17–20 you will find maps of the NHC and the rest of Will County identifying trail locations. Next is a summary table listing information such as trail length and type of surface for each site. More detailed information is provided in the individual sections. You'll learn how to get to each site, where to park, and what facilities are available such as bicycle racks, restrooms, and drinking fountains, as well as information about plants and animals living in or visiting the area.

Following the summary table, 22 sections describe trails and bike paths starting with the I&M Canal State Trail in Section 1. This trail is a linear pathway starting (or ending) at the western terminus of the I&M Canal in LaSalle/Peru in LaSalle County. The trail runs on the towpath of the old canal for 61 miles through LaSalle and Grundy Counties ending in Will County near Joliet. At the time of writing, construction was underway to complete the last 5.5 miles of the trail from I-55 to Brandon Road Lock and Dam southwest of Joliet. For the eastern third of the NHC, there is presently no single continuous trail. However, two new trails and an on-road bike route through Joliet are being developed at the time of writing. These will become part of the NHC backbone trail system. When completed, an additional 25 miles of trail and bike route will run from Joliet to Lyons in Cook County.

Sections 2 and 3 describe the scenic trails that meander through the beautiful canyons and bluffs of Starved Rock and Matthiessen State

A view of the Illinois River and Lover's Leap overlook from Starved Rock.

Parks in LaSalle County. Heading east, Sections 4 and 5 cover other state parks and natural areas in LaSalle and Grundy Counties along or near the Illinois River.

In Will County, not only the human population, but also the number of natural areas and off-road trails and bike paths are growing rapidly. Adding to some beautiful existing sites such as Kankakee River State Park (Section 6), new nature preserves are being established. The largest of which is the 19,500-acre Midewin National Tallgrass Prairie described in Section 7. At the time of writing, there were no trails open at Midewin. However, planning is underway for what hopefully will become an extensive trail system. Also, a new trail and on-street bike route are being developed in Joliet (Section 8). A 13.1-mile Old Plank Road Trail (Section 9) extending from Mokena in Will County to Park Forest in Cook County was recently completed. The new trail has been very well received by trail users and, as a result, 3.3 miles will be added to extend the trail to New Lenox in 1998, and 5 additional miles are planned to downtown Joliet. A historic trail through Lockport (Section 10) takes you along the I&M Canal and through the community past numerous canal points of interest. The Centennial

Trail (Section 11), under development, will extend 20 miles from the Gaylord Donnelley Canal Trail in Lockport to the Chicago Portage National Historic Site in Lyons. When completed, the NHC backbone trail system will run 88 miles from Lyons to LaSalle/Peru.

Sections 12–15 describe FPDWC trails at 15 sites including some beautiful preserves such as McKinley Woods, Hickory Creek Preserve, Messenger Woods, and Thorn Creek Nature Preserve.

Section 16 describes trails in Lemont and Romeoville followed by the only NHC trail site in DuPage County—scenic Waterfall Glen Forest Preserve (Section 17). Several Cook County sites are also part of the corridor. Lake Katherine Nature Preserve in Palos Heights, the 14,000-acre Palos Preserves, Cook County Forest Preserve District's I&M Canal Bicycle Trail, the Arie Crown Bicycle Trail, and trails along the Salt Creek Greenway are covered in Sections 18–21. The eastern terminus of the NHC at Navy Pier in downtown Chicago and walks along the Chicago River are briefly described in Section 22.

Following the narratives of the existing NHC and Will County trails and bike paths, Section 23 outlines greenway trail plans throughout Chicagoland and beyond. This includes the Grand Illinois Trail, which will extend 500+ miles from Chicagoland west to the Mississippi River, then north to Galena before looping back to Chicago. The target is to complete this massive trail system by the year 2000. You can hike and bike much of it today. Also included in Section 23 is the 6,300-mile American Discovery Trail currently under development. The Old Plank Road Trail and the I&M Canal State Trail are part of both these long distance trail systems.

Hiking

What we describe as hiking in this guidebook can encompass leisure walking as well as a brisk run. All the trails covered are open for hiking. The pathway might have an asphalt, crushed limestone, packed earth, or woodchip surface. As well as being peaceful places to visit, the forest, prairie, and meadow provide the hiker with oxygen given off by the trees and plants rather than the carbon monoxide and other pollutants generated on the streets and highways. Also the bird songs and insect chatter are more peaceful than traffic noise.

The NHC and the rest of Will County have trails to meet varying needs. Distances ranging from less than 1 mile to a 122-mile round-trip on the I&M Canal State Trail are available. A good place for a short hike with young children is at one of the nature or visitor centers located in many of the parks and preserves.

Biking

This guidebook focuses on off-road trails and bike paths. You can bicycle 5, 20, 50, 100, or more miles on trail systems such as the I&M Canal State Trail, the Old Plank Road Trail, the Palos Preserves trails and others. This guidebook describes how you can get from one trail system to another nearby pathway.

If you want to get the cyclist's perspective on the region's street system, the Chicagoland Bicycle Map is an excellent resource. Produced and sold by the Chicagoland Bicycle Federation (CBF), 312-42-PEDAL, the map recommends a regional network of on-street bike routes in addition to showing where the major off-road trails are. The CBF map includes the eastern portion of the NHC from the Joliet area to Chicago. Also the Illinois Department of Transportation (IDOT) has published a series of nine free Illinois Bicycle maps. Map 3 covers recommended on-road bike routes and off-road trails through the NHC from Will County to LaSalle County. The IDOT maps rate roads for "adult cyclists of average or better experience". Call IDOT on 217-782-0834 for more information.

Some forest preserve and nature center trails are closed for bicycling to protect the natural areas. The table beginning on page 22 shows which trails are open for bicycles. Be sure to comply with the trail-use signs at the trailheads.

Cross-country skiing

When the snow falls, you will find that most of the trails and bike paths described in this book are great places to cross-country ski.

Nature Centers

A highlight of the forest preserves, state parks, and other trail sites are the interpretive facilities provided at the many nature centers found throughout the NHC and the rest of Will County. You will usually find excellent hiking trails near the nature centers. As well as exhibits and displays, there are many programs offered throughout the year covering natural history, ecology, and wildlife. These sites are described in some detail in this guidebook.

Rules of the Trail

The popularity of off-road trails continues to grow. As a result, you may encounter bicyclists, runners, wheelchair users, hikers, equestrians, and in-line skaters. Please be considerate of others so that everyone can enjoy our trails. Safety suggestions and regulations to protect the environment are described on page 21. Please read them carefully. Check the signage on the trails for any site-specific trail rules.

Visitor Centers, Lodging, Calendar of Events, Organizations

In the appendices, we have included a listing of NHC visitor centers as well as nearby lodging, starting on page 165. Describing all the attractions and places of historical significance that comprise the NHC is beyond the scope of this book. Contact one of the visitor centers for more information. You can call the Heritage Corridor Convention and Visitors Bureau at 800-926-2262. For more information about the Will County Forest Preserves, call 815-727-8700 or visit one of the nature centers described in this guidebook.

Also included in the appendices is a listing of bike shops in the NHC and the rest of Will County. A monthly calendar of events includes annual NHC and Will County special events and activities. You will also find a listing of bicycling, environmental, and hiking organizations. Please notify us of any oversights for future issues. Our address is Roots & Wings, P. O. Box 167, Lake Forest, Illinois 60045.

Comments/Order Form

To improve future editions, your comments would be very much appreciated. A form is on page 175. We'd also like to know if you'd be interested in future guidebooks. Page 176 contains an order form for those who want to purchase additional copies of this book or the other four guidebooks in our Chicagoland hiking and biking series.

A Little History

Humans came to northern Illinois 11,000 years ago as the glaciers from our most recent Ice Age were retreating. These hunter-gatherers descended from people who crossed a huge land mass that once connected what is today Alaska and Siberia. They wandered south and east through spruce forests and wetlands pursuing bison, elk, and the now extinct woolly mammoth and mastodon. As the climate warmed, Indian tribes began hunting deer and waterfowl and gathering seeds and berries. Archaeological digs near Starved Rock showed evidence of their camp sites. The temperature warmed further making conditions perfect for the formation of the great expanse of prairies that once thrived in this region. Wandering tribes, by the 12th century, had settled into villages of earthen lodges and were planting squash, sunflowers, and other crops that grew in the fertile prairie soils. These peoples also traversed the plentiful rivers flowing through the region. Starved Rock, along the Illinois River, became a favorite trading spot.

In 1673, two French explorers, Louis Jolliet and Father Marquette, ventured into this area, pursuing a passage from the Great Lakes to the Pacific. Instead, they found a link to the Mississippi and the Gulf of Mexico. On their return to Lake Michigan some friendly Native Americans guided them to a shortcut via a portage from the Des Plaines River to the South Branch of the Chicago River. French fur traders soon followed the same route seeking beaver pelts that would be made into hats for European gentlemen. As you hike or bike the Centennial Trail in Will County, you can visit the Isle a la Cache Museum in Romeoville to learn more about the lives of French voyagers who plied the nearby Des Plaines 300 years ago.

Vision of a Canal

Jolliet was the first to recognize that a canal could connect the Great Lakes with the Des Plaines and Illinois Rivers. But with the isolation of the area plus British competition for the French fur trade, neither the French nor the British chose to take on such a project.

After the American Revolution, the new federal government negotiated a treaty with the Northwest Territory Indians who ceded land at the mouth of the Chicago River to the United States. Fort Dearborn was built there. Meanwhile, many settlers had already worked their way west of the Appalachian Mountains to this area. By 1810, the Federal Congress was talking about building a canal to provide transportation between the East Coast and the Mississippi. In 1816, a second treaty with the Potowatami gave 10 miles of land on both sides of the Des Plaines and Illinois Rivers from the Fox River to the Chicago lake shore to the federal government. In 1819, the Illinois Territory became a state. Following the Blackhawk War of 1832, the Potowatami ceded the whole region to the United States. Settlers began migrating farther north into the vast prairies and river valleys of northern Illinois. They also found trails used by the Native Americans such as the Ottawa Trail, today known as Joliet Road.

In 1835, a canal commission was established. Will County was established in 1836 and construction began on the Illinois and Michigan (I&M) Canal. William Gooding, an experienced canal

Gebhard Woods State Park.

builder, was appointed Chief Engineer. A 60-foot-wide, 6-foot-deep, 97-mile long canal was planned; however, a national Depression first slowed and then stopped construction in 1841 due to a lack of funds.

In 1837, John Deere had invented the steel plow which effectively broke through the thick turf of the tall grass prairie exposing the fertile soil below. Land was available for $1.25 an acre. Settlers established homesteads and plowed the prairie. Corn and other crops flourished in the rich prairie soil. But there was no good way to transport the farmer's produce to the East Coast markets. There were no railroads. Dirt roads were slow or impassable a good part of the year for the heavily loaded wagons. Plank roads helped, but not much. The time had finally come to complete the canal.

In 1845, construction began again. The canal was finished in 1848. The building of the I&M Canal was hard and dangerous work. Each year many of the Irish and other immigrant workers died mostly from disease. They built a magnificent system of 15 locks, aqueducts, bridges, dams and a 97-mile long dirt trail called the towpath. The locks lifted the barges and boats heading east and lowered them heading west. Mules led by men or boys called "hoagies" walked the towpath pulling the canal boats. Barges brought finished goods from the East and transported corn and wheat back to the East Coast. Packets provided passengers with a more comfortable ride than the bumpy and dusty stagecoaches.

Population growth in Chicago and the communities along the canal exploded. From 1848 to 1857, Chicago's population increased 600%. Ironically the canal's heyday was short-lived. In the 1850's, railroad lines appeared on the scene. Nonetheless, the canal's traffic continued growing, finally peaking in the early 1880s. By then an extensive railroad network was in place. The death knell for the I&M Canal came in 1900 when the much larger Chicago Sanitary & Ship Canal was opened. The I&M Canal stayed in business, mostly for pleasure boat traffic, until 1933. That same year the Civilian Conservation Corps began work on shelters and other improvements to the parks and preserves along the old canal.

Since its closure, the once grand 60-to-120-foot-wide canal has shrunk to a narrow and shallow remnant of its former self due to erosion and natural filling of sedimentation as well as human construction and development. As you hike and bike the trails, stop at the visitor centers along the way to learn more about the canal and its colorful history. On the trails, note the locks, aqueducts, and buildings that not so long ago were part of the bustling traffic on the I&M Canal.

I&M Canal National Heritage Corridor, Trail Sites in LaSalle and Grundy Counties

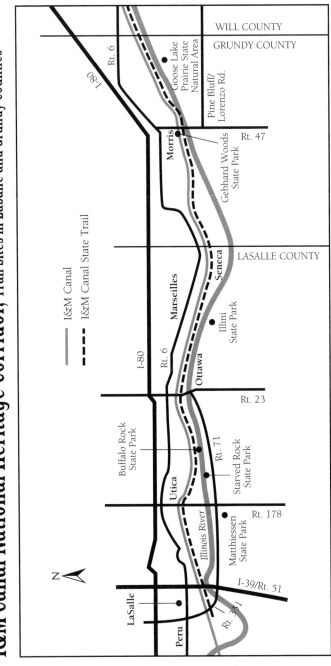

WILL COUNTY

GRUNDY COUNTY

LASALLE COUNTY

N

Rt. 6

I-80

Goose Lake Prairie State Natural Area

Pine Bluff/ Lorenzo Rd.

Morris

Gebhard Woods State Park

Rt. 47

Seneca

Marseilles

Illini State Park

Ottawa

Rt. 23

I-80

Rt. 6

Buffalo Rock State Park

Utica

Rt. 71

Starved Rock State Park

Illinois River

Rt. 178

Matthiessen State Park

I-39/Rt. 51

LaSalle

Peru

Rt. 351

—— I&M Canal

– – – I&M Canal State Trail

Will County Trail Sites (Including I&M Canal NHC)

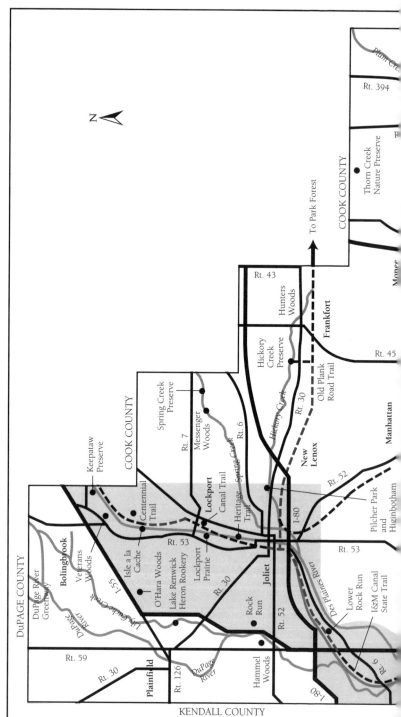

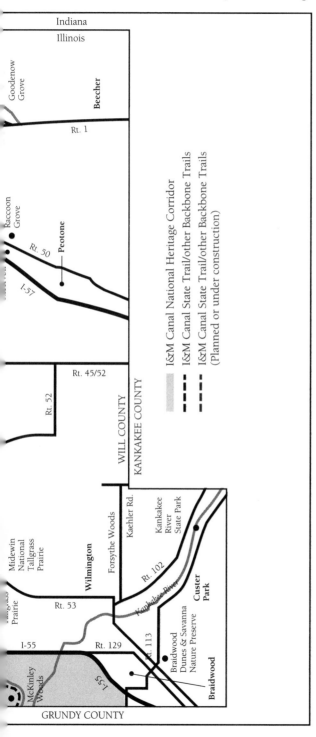

I&M Canal National Heritage Corridor, Trail Sites in Cook and DuPage Counties

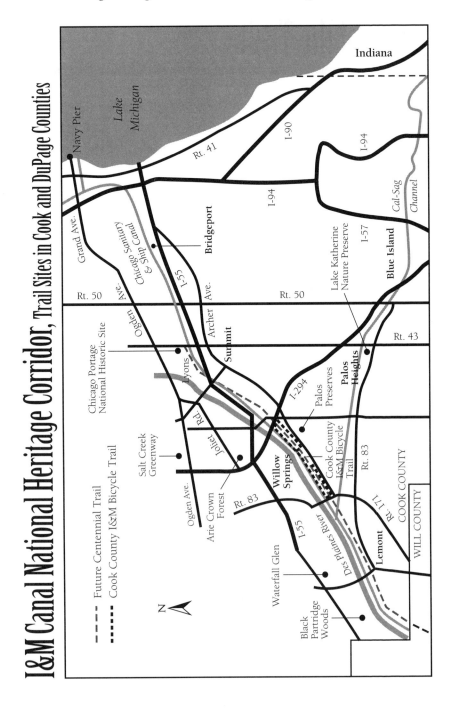

Rules of the Trail

- Leave nature as you find it for others to enjoy. Remain on the trail.
- Deposit litter in proper receptacles.
- Leash all pets. (Some preserves do not allow pets.)
- Be alert for cars or bicycles. Stay to the right.
- Don't feed the wildlife.
- Will County Forest Preserves are open from 8 a.m. to 10 p. m. April–October and from 8 a.m. to 5 p.m. November–March. Call the other sites for hours of operation.
- Don't wear earphones. You can't hear a bicyclist coming.
- Relax, have fun, and enjoy!
- Check for ticks when you're finished.

Specific for Bicyclists
- Wear a helmet.
- Be alert for loose gravel, debris, holes, or bumps on the trails.
- Take it easy with hikers of all ages on the trail.
- Ride in single file.
- Cautiously pass hikers and equestrians on the left. Call out "passing on the left". But remember the hiker may be deaf or hard of hearing or may be wearing earphones.
- Keep both hands on your handle bars.
- Keep to designated bike trails in the forest preserves, state parks, and other natural areas.
- See "Illinois Bicycle Rules" for additional safety information for on-road bicycling.

For your enjoyment
- Apply insect repellent before you go out depending on the season.
- Take water on long hikes or bike rides.

Illinois & Michigan National Heritage Corridor and Will County Hiking and Biking Trails

Park, Preserve, or Trail	Section	Miles–Hike	/Bike	Surface	Author's Comments
I&M Canal State Trail	1	61*	61*	L	Continuous trail along the canal from Joliet to LaSalle/Peru.
Starved Rock State Park	2	13*	—	P, S	Beautiful canyons, scenic bluff views, super trails. Very hilly. An increasing percentage of trails are covered by boardwalk.
Matthiessen State Park	3	5	—	P, G	Mile-long canyon. Adjoins Starved Rock but more secluded.
Buffalo Rock State Park & the Effigy Tumuli	4	2.5	—	P, G	Scenic vistas of Illinois River and largest earthen sculpture since Mt. Rushmore.
Illini State Park		1.8	—	P	Popular camping site along the Illinois River.
Goose Lake Prairie State Natural Area	5	7	—	L, G	2500+ acre prairie.
Kankakee River State Park	6	17.5*	10.5*	A, L, P	Beautiful sandstone cliffs along the river and waterfall on Rock Creek.
Midewin National Tallgrass Prairie	7	*	*	*	Trail planning is underway at this 19,500-acre site.
Joliet Trails	8				
Joliet Iron Works Historic Site		3.7*	2.7*	L, C	1-mile interpretive hiking trail and 2.7-mile multi-use Heritage Trail which is part of NHC backbone route.
Joliet On-Road Bike Route		—	3	A	Designated and marked bike route connects to I&M Canal State Trail.
Will-Joliet Bicentennial Park		.5	.5	B	Beautiful murals and brick riverwalk.
Pilcher Park		5	3	P, A G	Maple and oak forest along Hickory Creek. Excellent nature center.
Higinbotham Woods		.3	—	P	Remnants of Native American mounds.
Old Plank Road Trail	9	13.1*	13.1*	A	From Park Forest to Mokena. A 3.3-mile extension to New Lenox is scheduled for 1998. An additional 4.7 miles to downtown Joliet is planned.

Park, Preserve, or Trail	Section	Miles–Hike/Bike		Surface	Author's Comments
Lockport Trails	10				
Gaylord Donnelley Canal Trail		2.5	2.5	A, L	Visit the NHC Visitor Center in the Gaylord Building.
Dellwood Park		2	2	A, G	Once a popular amusement park.
Centennial Trail	11	20*	20*	L	NHC backbone trail currently under development from the portage site in Lyons to Lockport. Three miles open in Will County.
Southwestern Will County Forest Preserve District Hiking Trails	12				
McKinley Woods		2.5	—	P	Upland trails and access to the I&M Canal State Trail.
Forsythe Woods		2	—	P	Woodland trails near Wilmington.
Braidwood Dunes & Savanna Nature Preserve		1.2	—	P	Dunesland and oak savanna.
Northwestern Will County Forest Preserve District Trails	13				
Keepataw Prairie		.3	—	P	Bluff view of Des Plaines River Valley.
Veterans Woods		.3	—	P	Short ravine trail.
Lake Renwick Heron Rookery Nature Preserve		.2	—	G	Illinois Nature Preserve featuring a multitude of herons and egrets. Guided tours only.
Lockport Prairie Nature Preserve		.4	—	P	Illinois Nature Preserve along the Des Plaines.
Rock Run Preserve-Black Road Access		2*	1.2*	A, L	Interpretive trails through sedge meadow and prairie. Greenway trail extension planned for 1998-99.
Lower Rock Run I&M Canal Access		.4	.2	A, L	New preserve provides wildlife observation area and direct access to I&M Canal State Trail.
Hammel Woods		3	—	P	Beautiful bluff trail along the DuPage River.

Park, Preserve, or Trail	Section	Miles–Hike/Bike		Surface	Author's Comments
North Central Will County Forest Preserve District Trails	14				
Hickory Creek Preserve		3.7*	1.8*	A, P	Largest forest preserve in Will County. Woodland and meadow trails as well as access to Old Plank Road Trail.
Messenger Woods Nature Preserve		2	—	P	Illinois Nature Preserve. Beautiful spring wildflowers.
Spring Creek Preserve		3.2	—	L, M, P	Equestrian trail open for hiking..
Eastern Will County Forest Preserve District Trails	15				
Goodenow Grove Forest Preserve		3.5	—	P, G	Nature center, woodland trails and family camping.
Monee Reservoir		2.3	.3	M, A	Wetlands and free fishing lake.
Raccoon Grove Nature Preserve		.5	—	P	Illinois Nature Preserve.
Thorn Creek Woods Nature Preserve		2.5	—	P	Illinois Nature Preserve with secluded trails. Pine grove.
Lemont and Romeoville Trails	16				
Lemont's I&M Canal Trail		3.4*	3.4*	L	Trail improvements planned. Will connect with Centennial Trail.
Black Partridge Forest Preserve		.5	—	P	Spring wildflowers.
O'Hara Woods Nature Preserve		3	—	P	Rustic trail through maple and oak woodland
Waterfall Glen Forest Preserve	17	9.5*	9.5*	L, M	Narrow side trails open to hikers only. Multi-use trails open to equestrians.
Lake Katherine Nature Preserve	18	3.5	—	W	Community of Palos Heights turned a 158-acre dumping ground into a beautiful natural habitat.

Park, Preserve, or Trail	Section	Miles–Hike/Bike		Surface	Author's Comments
Palos Preserves	19				14,000 acres of wilderness. Premier spot for hiking and biking
Multi-use Trails		35	35	P, L	Open to equestrians.
Little Red Schoolhouse Nature Center		3	—	P, L	Nature exhibits and trails through oak forests.
Camp Sagawau		6.2	—	M	Only natural rock canyon in Cook County. Open for guided tours.
Cook County's I&M Canal Bicycle Trail	20	8.9	8.9	A	Good spot for beginning bicyclists. Straight path with only one road crossing.
Arie Crown Forest Bicycle Trail		3.2	3.2	P	Woodland trail through rolling terrain.
Salt Creek Greenway	21	*	*		
Bemis Woods Preserve Trail		3	3	P	Multi-use trail. Open to equestrians.
Salt Creek Bicycle Trail		6.6	6.6	A	Bicycle trail along the creek from Bemis Woods to Brookfield Zoo.
Wolf Road Prairie		2	—	C, M	88 acres of native prairie and oak savanna at this Illinois Nature Preserve.
Navy Pier and Chicago River Walks	22	—	—	A, C	Lake Michigan gateway to the I&M Canal National Heritage Corridor.
Nearby Trails	23				
The Grand Illinois Trail		500+*	500+*		Currently under development. Will run through 18 counties from Navy Pier to the Mississippi River to Galena back to Chicago. Listed below are two nearby sections.
Kaskaskia/Alliance Trail		13*	13*		Planned trail will connect from I&M Canal State Trail in Peru to Bureau Junction. Partially on local roads.
Hennepin Canal State Trail		59*	59*	L, M	Bureau Junction–Green Rock. Crushed limestone trail planned.

Notes:
1.) Surface designations: A-asphalt, C-concrete, G-gravel, L-crushed limestone, M- mowed turf, P-packed earth, S-sand, W-woodchip. A mountain or hybrid bike is more effective on a gravel, mowed turf, packed earth, or woodchip trail.
2.) Cross-country skiing in the winter is welcomed except for those trails designated hiking only.
3.)*Signifies additional trails under construction or planned.

The Illinois and Michigan Canal State Trail

The backbone of the I&M Canal National Heritage Corridor (NHC) trail system is the 61-mile state trail that runs along the south side of the canal from Brandon Road Lock and Dam southwest of Joliet to LaSalle/Peru at Route 351. The multi-use hiking and biking trail had an earlier life as the tow path for the drivers who guided horses and mules along the canal embankment. They pulled barges laden with grain and corn east to Lake Michigan, for transportation to the East Coast. Meanwhile west-bound barges returned the favor with finished goods and products manufactured in the East for use by the farmers and settlers in the rapidly growing Midwest.

You will discover interesting places along the way as you pass through the communities of Channahon, Morris, Seneca, Marseilles, Ottawa, Utica, and LaSalle. Several state parks (Channahon, W. G. Stratton, Gebhard Woods, and Buffalo Rock) as well as Will County Forest Preserves (McKinley Woods and Lower Rock Run) offer easy access to the state trail. Nearby are numerous other beautiful natural areas such as Starved Rock and Matthiessen State

Parks and the 19,500-acre Midewin National Tallgrass Prairie currently under development.

The trail, owned and maintained by the Illinois Department of Natural Resources (DNR), is a crushed limestone surface. It is relatively flat and straight, like the nearby canal. The pathway is well-maintained and in good shape. However you will encounter washouts and loose gravel in a few spots. Go slowly if you are biking. Also you will see more wildlife and enjoy nature.

Bring plenty of water and snacks as well as insect repellent in the summer. As mentioned above, several communities, forest preserves, and state parks are adjacent to the trail where you can find food and drink as well as restrooms. However there are quite a few miles between some of them. Several trail access sites are described in detail in this section. Also see the map and text for mileage between sites. Most trail users will not ride or hike the entire 61-mile trail in one visit. The wonderful thing is that you may hike as much or as little of the trail as you choose, from 1 mile to 122 miles round-trip. In fact, soon you will be able to venture much farther on connecting trails throughout Northern Illinois and eventually across the entire country. More on that later.

DNR has provided several camping sites along the trail and will be adding more. Good places to leave your car overnight are Channahon State Park, McKinley Woods (a Will County forest preserve), and Gebhard Woods State Park.

Let's take a 61-mile trip down the trail starting at Brandon Road Lock and Dam, the northern trailhead, and ending near the canal boat basin in LaSalle. The first 5.5 miles from Brandon Road to I-55 was under construction at the time of writing. By the time you read this book, the trail addition should be completed.

Brandon Road Lock and Dam and Brandon Road are on the outskirts of Joliet. The trailhead is north of Route 6 off of Brandon Road. Today a massive lock and dam system operates south of Route 6 as part of the Illinois Waterway System. You can drive south of Route 6 to the visitors area to see the lock. Maybe you will get to observe the system in operation transporting a passing barge. Approximately 45,000 tons of freight move through the Brandon Locks daily.

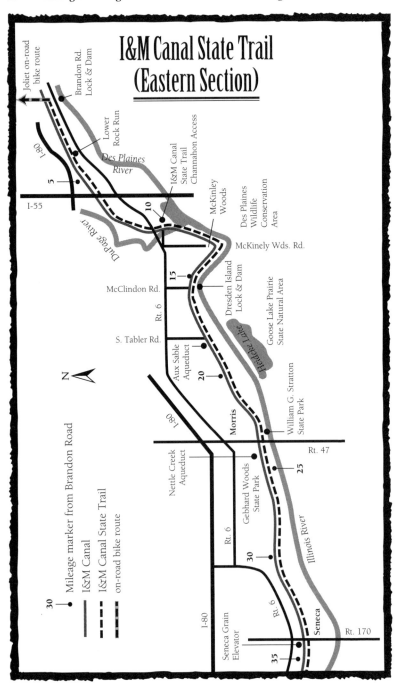

I&M Canal State Trail
(Eastern Section)

How to get to Brandon Road Lock and Dam:

Take I-80, I-55, or Routes 6, 30, 52, 53, or 59 to Joliet. From I-80, take the Larkin Avenue exit south to Route 6 (Channahon Road). Turn left heading northeast to Brandon Road. Turn left on Brandon and then left again on Mound Road. A new trailhead parking area is planned at Mound. On bike, take the designated on-road bike route through downtown Joliet. (See Section 8.)

The trail runs south of and near the I&M Canal which becomes a separate waterway again near Brandon Lock. In Joliet the canal shares a common channel with the Des Plaines River. The trail runs north of Route 6 and the river. Across the Des Plaines is the 19,500-acre Midewin National Tallgrass Prairie. An underpass at Bush Road is the only road crossing over the 5.5 mile section to I-55. The trail passes by gravel mining operations with tall hills of sand and gravel left by the last glacier. Excavations have been underway in this somewhat isolated area since the mid-19th Century.

The Forest Preserve District of Will County has recently opened a new preserve. Currently called Rock Run I&M Canal Access, the preserve lives up to its name by providing the only direct access to the I&M Canal State Trail between Brandon Road and Channahon. (See below.) I&M Canal Access is approximately 3.5 miles from the eastern trailhead at Brandon Road. Extensive parking for trail users as well as a wildlife observation area, picnic tables, a large shelter, water, and restrooms are available. The forest preserve district is restoring prairie and woodland at the site. (See Section 13 for more information.)

How to get to Rock Run I&M Canal Access:

Take I-55 north of I-80 to the Jefferson Street exit. Head east on Jefferson to Houbolt Avenue. Turn right (south). Proceed south for 3.1 miles passing under I-80. (Houbolt becomes Bush Road south of I-80.) The preserve entrance is to your right. From the south, you can take Route 6 to Bush Road, then north to the entrance.

At 5.5 miles out from Brandon Road you will pass under I-55. Farmland gives way to a forest south of the trail. Two does appeared, ran down the path for a bit, then disappeared into the woods as I passed by. Here the canal is like a lagoon—much wider than before.

The trail runs on a ridge about 12 feet above the canal. Near Channahon an underpass comes into view. Duck! There is limited clearance. The path runs along a residential area with a road crossing at Knapp Street before entering Channahon State Park (at 9.3 miles out). This is a good spot for a break. Water, shelters, picnic tables, restrooms, and a public telephone are available. Check out I&M Canal Lock #6 on the east side and Lock #7 on the west side of the spillway as well as the original locktender's house. Also note the American Discovery Trail sign on a bench near the lock. The I&M Canal State Trail is part of a 6,300-mile national trail system currently under development.

The name Channahon is a Native American word for "the meeting of the waters". Here the Des Plaines and the DuPage Rivers converge. In July 1996, the convergence became a collision. Torrential rainfall along the DuPage to the north resulted in a deluge that came crashing into the canal. Two hundred feet of canal embankment, the spillway dam for the DuPage River, and a trail bridge were destroyed. As a result, the section of the I&M Canal from Channahon to Morris was without water. Reconstruction of the spillway, the canal embankment, and construction of a new trail bridge over the spillway were completed in late 1997. Some good came from this million dollar project. The DNR was able to do some dredging to remove sedimentation buildup as well as to clean up the canal bed. Also a packet and other boats long buried beneath the water and mud of the canal were discovered.

Camping along the trail is available at Channahon State Park. You can also leave your car in the parking lot for overnight hiking and biking excursions. Call 815-467-4271 to make arrangements.

How to get to Channahon State Park:

Take I-55 south of I-80 to U. S. Route 6 (Exit #248). Head west 2.7 miles to the community of Channahon. Turn left at Canal Street. Proceed .4 mile to Story Street. Turn right into the state park parking area and trail access.

South of Channahon, the trail runs along farmland north of the canal. My first clue (through the power of deductive reasoning) was the presence of five cows standing knee-deep in the canal on a hot

Jill Bergstrom, Courtesy Illinois Department of Natural Resources

I&M Canal State Trail.

July day. The Des Plaines River appears on the scene startlingly wide here, particularly for a Chicagoland resident like me who is used to narrow rivers. A great white egret stood silently on a tree limb in the river looking for lunch. Occasional stone overlooks (near Moose Island) provide scenic vistas along the waterway. Across the river, a marina, some homes, and a water filtration plant line the bank.

Farther south, a woodland separates the trail from the river. The canal contained little water here during my summer visit. But there were a lot of logs in the canal bed. At 12.3 miles out, at a big bend in the canal and the river, you will come to the entrance to McKinley Woods, a Will County forest preserve. Take the bridge across the canal at Boatsman Landing. This beautiful preserve has excellent hiking trails as well as water, restrooms, picnic tables, shelters, and camping facilities. This is also a good place to park for a day trip or overnight. (See Section 12 for more information about McKinley Woods.)

How to get to McKinley Woods:

From the east take Route 6 southwest from I-55. Proceed through

Channahon, over the DuPage River, and up a steep hill to McKinley Woods Road. Head left 2 miles past a water tower, cornfields, and through the Highlands, an upscale residential community. The entrance to McKinley Woods is at the end of the road. From the west, take Route 6 east of Route 47 to McKinley Woods Road.

As I traveled south on the state trail, I heard the sound of a helicopter, which temporarily overwhelmed the birds and insects. Apparently inspecting electrical power facilities along the trail, the helicopter pilot went north, and the sounds of nature returned. Here the canal bed becomes a mud flat. On the cracked earth surface of the canal occasional soda cans, tires or clam shells are evident. When the water drained out of the canal bed in 1996, the clams became easy prey for birds. By the time you read this, water will be returned to the canal between Channahon and Morris. West of McKinley Woods the Des Plaines converges with the Kankakee River, which flows northeast from Kankakee County, to form the Illinois River.

Soon you will see a large facility across the river. The Dresden Nuclear Power Plant, one of the first nuclear power generating stations in the world, has been in operation since 1960. At 15.3 miles out is the Dresden Island Lock & Dam. Parking is available here. Take the short path to the left to see the lock and dam. Across the canal you can glimpse the remains of the small village of Dresden: a red barn, a former inn, and a cemetery. Here the Rutherford Tavern once slaked the thirst of many canal and stagecoach travelers.

How to get to Dresden Island Lock & Dam:

Take Route 6 west of Channahon to McClindon Road. Head south to the parking area.

Continuing west, the path is shady with woodlands lining the trail. After two underpasses and a road crossing at South Taber Road, you will come to the Aux Sable Aqueduct at 17.7 miles out. Here the Aux Sable Creek, on its way to the Illinois River, crosses the canal. Originally a wood and stone aqueduct was constructed over the creek to carry the canal waters farther west. More recently the original structure was replaced with a steel aqueduct. You will also find Lock #8 and an old locktender's residence west of the aqueduct. The locktender had to be available 24 hours-a-day, 7 days-a-week to respond to the sound of a horn announcing the impending arrival of a barge or packet. A one-room schoolhouse, a boarding house, blacksmith, saw mill, and of course, a distillery were in operation here as well. While not visible or accessible from the trail, two miles south of the canal, across the river, are two large sites, Goose Lake Prairie State Natural Area and Heidecke Lake (see Section 5).

West of Aux Sable, the trail leads through a wetland and then a dense woodland. Cemetery Road parallels the trail from Dresden to Morris. A pullout camping site with grill is left of the path at 21.1 miles out. The DNR plans to add more of these spots along the trail. Another trail parking area can be found east of Morris at Armstrong Street. Residences line the canal to the north as you enter the community of Morris. The wide Illinois River rejoins the canal trail here. In warm weather, you will hear the sound of jet skis at William G. Stratton State Park long before the river is visible. You will find plenty of parking here, benches, restrooms, and a water fountain (23.1 miles out). A restaurant along the river unfortunately was closed on my visits. Here the trail passes under busy Route 47. West of the Route 47 bridge is a much smaller iron trail bridge that crosses the canal and leads to Canal Point Plaza in downtown Morris, the Grundy County seat. Nearby are several restaurants and a grocery store if you need food and drink as I did.

As you leave downtown Morris, the canal is once again filled with water. A wooden bridge leads to a residential area west of town. Nearby stands a large grain storage facility. Continuing west you will soon come to an old stone aqueduct over Nettle Creek at Gebhard Woods State Park (24.4 miles out). West of the aqueduct is a trail bridge that takes you across the canal into the state park. Walk through this picturesque park and along Nettle Creek to enjoy an abundance of wildlife. You will discover moisture-loving trees such as silver maples, cottonwoods, and sycamores close to the shore line. Farther away grow hardwoods such as black walnut and oak. Before these trees regain their leaves in spring, a host of wildflowers blankets the forest floor. Reaching for the sunlight before the trees shade them are trout lilies with their lovely white flowers, the taller phlox with bluish-pink flowers, and white trilliums, with their showy three white petals that fade to pink as the season progresses.

The creek also attracts wood ducks. The male of this species dons a crest and a face that looks as if it had been painted with green, white, yellow, and red strokes. Look for signs of beaver too. Gnawed tree trunks with light-colored shavings on the ground indicate that a beaver may have been active the night before. In the winter, you can also search for mink, opossum, and fox tracks in the snow.

How to get to Gebhard Woods State Park:

From I-80, take Route 47 south into downtown Morris. Head west on Jefferson Street which becomes Freemont Avenue. Turn left on Ottawa Street 1 mile west of Route 47.

At Gebhard Woods, north of the trail, you will find a large tent camping area, water, a state park office (10 a.m. to 4 p.m. daily), a public telephone, shelters, picnic tables, and restrooms. This is an excellent spot for a break given that the next refueling point along the trail is Seneca 10 miles farther west.

Gebhard is also a good spot if you want to leave your vehicle overnight. You need to notify the DNR personnel at the park office if you intend to do so. Also at Gebhard you will find the .8-mile Nettle Creek Nature Trail. The nature trail is a hiking-only packed earth surfaced pathway that winds through stately oak trees and along the creek. Also a crushed limestone trail runs for a short distance along the north side of the canal east to Nettle Creek and the aqueduct. An information sign post indicates the distance to points of interest.

Continuing west of Morris, Old Stage Road parallels the trail and canal to the north. Corn fields, woodlands, and wetlands, with an occasional residence, line the trail. Benches every few miles provide resting spots. Watch for loose gravel in this section. The trail leads through a picturesque tunnel of trees here as it does in many spots along the way. Woodlands on both sides of the trail with overhanging foliage also provide cooling shade on hot summer days. While there have been many acres of farmland along the pathway, I was pleasantly surprised that most of the surrounding environment is woods and wetlands. Here the canal water is filled with duckweed presenting a

Jill Bergstrom, Courtesy Illinois Department of Natural Resources

Bicyclists on the trail near Gebhard Woods.

green pea soup appearance to the trail user as well as a meal to dabbling ducks. A short asphalt side road along a neighborhood serves as the pathway entering Seneca.

The trail crosses Main Street in Seneca (34.5 miles out). A convenience food store is south of the trail. Other restaurants are nearby. A shelter with picnic tables is a good spot for a break. A remnant of the canal's glory days looms above the canal west of Main Street. The 65-foot-tall Seneca grain elevator was opened for business in 1862. After the farmer's grain was weighed on a scale, a steam-powered hydraulic lift dumped the wagon's contents in a hopper where buckets on a conveyor belt lifted the grain to storage bins. The historic, but presently dilapidated, grain elevator is being restored.

West of Seneca, the water filled canal is 10-to-15-feet wide for a distance and then suddenly dry again. Route 6 parallels the trail to the north into Marseilles. You will encounter a few curves and small hills on the trail path between Seneca and Ottawa. Caution signs point out upcoming curves. Between Seneca and Marseilles, you will pass several large manufacturing facilities including a phosphate feed

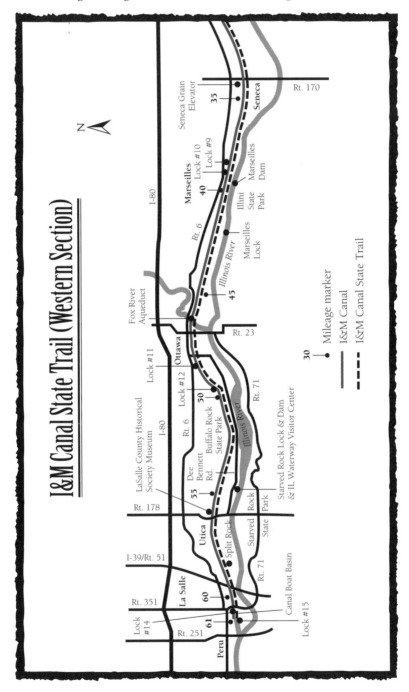

I&M Canal State Trail (Western Section)

products operation and a chemical plant.

Industry came early to Marseilles. Flour and paper mills were operating in mid-19th Century followed by many other manufacturing facilities. As you approach downtown, you will pass Locks #9 and #10. Except for the locks there is little evidence left that the canal was a major part of life in early Marseilles. Slightly indented mowed grass areas are all that are left. The trail leads through two underpasses including one under Main Street 39.9 miles out. Watch for glass on the trail here.

For an interesting side trip, take the pedestrian crossing on the new Main Street bridge south across the rapids in the Illinois River to Illini State Park. The Marseilles Lock and Dam is west of the 510-acre state park. (See Section 4 for more information.)

Heading west leaving Marseilles, the trail leads through another woodland. Here the canal looks more like a mountain stream with water flowing around stones deposited on the canal bed. A wild turkey was strolling along the trail as I passed by. In no big hurry to leave the scene, he (or she) sauntered into the forest along the trail. Wild turkeys once proliferated this area, feasting on the plentiful acorns available in oak savannas. Recent reintroduction of this species has been successful. A lucky observer today may even spot a train of young turkeys following their parents in single-file fashion along the trail.

Note the numerous caution signs here with several curvy sections, small bridge crossings, and loose gravel. At 46.3 miles out, you will come to the Fox River Aqueduct. When built in the 1830s, the original wood and stone aqueduct was 320-feet-long consisting of eight 40-foot spans. Locals considered the aqueduct the eighth wonder of the world. Today a metal aqueduct for the canal parallels the trail bridge crossing over the Fox. When the canal was built, separate bridges were constructed for the canal and wagon traffic. The Fox is the last of the Chicagoland rivers to join the Illinois on its journey to the Mississippi.

Following a road crossing (high curbs) and two underpasses, the trail enters a residential neighborhood on the east side of Ottawa, the LaSalle County seat. South of the trail in downtown Ottawa on Route 23 is the Reddick Mansion. Here the first Lincoln-Douglas debate was held. The downtown area is nicely restored. A trail parking area called Ottawa Access (48.4 miles out) is along Boyce Memorial Drive, which honors W. D. Boyce, the founder of the Boy Scouts of America who lived in Ottawa.

Sand deposits west of town did much to help Ottawa become a thriving community in the mid-19th and early 20th centuries. The lack of iron in the sand here made it ideal for glass-making. In the early 1900s, Ottawa was the leading glass producer in the world! You will pass a huge sand hill and the Ottawa Silica Company along the trail. You will also pass Lock #11 and #12 west of Ottawa. Note the limestone cliffs north of the trail. Such cliffs are noticeable a good part of the rest of the way to LaSalle.

Dee Bennett Road parallels the canal to the south and leads to the Illinois Waterway Visitors Center. There is no direct access from the trail.

At 51.2 miles out, you will come to the Buffalo Rock Access Area. Here, along Dee Bennett Road is a large paved parking area for trail users. Across the road is the entrance to Buffalo Rock State Park and the Effigy Tumuli. (See Section 4 for more information.) If you hear popping sounds nearby, yes that is gunfire. No, they are not shooting in your direction. The gunfire sounds come from a firing range north of the trail.

Southwest of Buffalo Rock is Blue Lake. The water is a beautiful turquoise color due to the salt deposits from the nearby silica mines. Three camping sites are available at pull-offs along the trail. West of Blue Lake is a large wetland on both sides of the trail. Here the canal loses its contained linear nature and becomes part of the extensive wetland. Noticing the 10-foot-tall reeds overwhelming the landscape, I expected to see Humphrey Bogart in the water pulling the African Queen with Katherine Hepburn aboard. For those of you under 40, consult your nearest video store or library video section if this allusion is meaningless.

Approaching Utica, the trail widens and has an asphalt surface since it also serves as an access road for a farm and residence. At 56.4 miles out, you will enter the community of Utica. Proceed straight up the small hill at the Utica Elevator Company. Take the pedestrian bridge across the canal. The LaSalle County Historical Society Museum is on Route 178 north of the trail. Starved Rock and Matthiessen State Parks are south of here. (See Sections 2 and 3.) After crossing Route 178, take a second pedestrian bridge south to pick up the trail heading west. Note the large stone memorial to local volunteers who helped restore this section of the canal from Utica to LaSalle.

West of Utica, the canal is much wider, approximately 30-feet wide, and filled with more duckweed. The CSXT railroad tracks parallel the trail and canal to the north.

At 58.8 miles out, you will come to limestone cliffs on both sides of the trail. Split Rock is an excellent example of the effort and danger involved in building the canal. To clear a passageway, workers used dangerous black powder to blast holes in the limestone cliff. Dynamite had not yet been invented. North of the canal, a 150-foot tunnel was created for the Rock Island Railroad. Also at this site the Illinois Traction System, an electric passenger rail line, ran from Joliet to Starved Rock in the early 20th century.

As I headed west on the trail, a large turtle basked in the sun atop one of many fallen limbs. I turned my bike around to get a closer look, but the turtle jumped into water. Later on my trip back east, I watched for the turtle and found two sunning themselves on fallen branches in the canal. They both quickly retreated into the water. As many as 50 painted turtles have been observed on a single log, often stacked atop each other in several layers. Even hatchlings can be seen basking. Basking in the sun serves several purposes. The heat maintains the preferred body temperature and the sun's ultraviolet helps eliminate skin parasites. The rays also help the turtles synthesize vitamins.

As you approach LaSalle, what appears to be the Illinois River is actually Split Rock Lake. Continuing west, two huge bridges cross the canal and the Illinois River. The first is for U. S. Route 39 and Route 51. One last aqueduct west of the bridge crosses Little Vermilion Creek. You will soon come to the bridge for Route 351.

For those of you keeping count, Lock #13 was mostly removed prior to DNR ownership. Remnants can be seen in extremely low water about 30 yards west of the earthen dam between Utica and LaSalle.

At 61 miles out is the western trailhead near restored Lock #14. Picnic tables and a parking area are nearby. Restrooms are at the top of the stairs, which lead to downtown LaSalle. Peru is to the west.

How to get to the western trailhead in LaSalle:

Take Route 351 south of I-80 at the LaSalle exit. Turn right on Route 6. Head west to Joliet Street. Head south (left) on Joliet 5 blocks to Canal Street. Head west (right) a short distance to the parking area entrance.

To the west is submerged Lock #15, which is not visible from the trailhead. Nearby are the steamboat and canal boat basins. Here steamers transferred their cargo to the barges for their trip up the 97-mile canal to Chicago.

As well as the camping opportunities mentioned earlier in this section, there are many lodging choices near the trail. See page 165 in the Appendix for a listing.

The I&M Canal State Trail serves as a key component in two emerging long-distance trail systems currently being developed. You'll see symbols and signage along the way identifying the 500+ mile Grand Illinois Trail that loops through northern Illinois and the 6,300-mile American Discovery Trail that runs from Cape Henlopen State Park in Delaware to Point Reyes National Seashore north of San Francisco. Both trail systems are described in more detail in Section 23.

The I&M Canal State Trail is open for cross-country skiing in winter. Call the DNR at 815-942-0796 for more information about the trail.

Starved Rock State Park

Bluffs and canyons and ravines. OH MY ! Borrowing a phrase from Dorothy helps describe the 13 miles of hiking trails winding through 18 magnificent stream-fed canyons, following the wide Illinois River, and climbing the high bluffs surrounding the sandstone canyons. If you are looking for flat pathways of asphalt, this is not the place for you. But if you want a place to hike with challenging climbs, gorgeous views from overlooks high above the river, and beautiful woodlands where bluebells flourish in spring, this is definitely the place for you. This wondrous collection of canyons, bluffs, and buttes was formed by melting glaciers sculpting the sandstone laid down in the Silurian Sea 420 million years ago.

It is somewhat ironic that motorists on busy I-80, less than four miles north of Starved Rock, pass through endless miles of rolling fields of corn and wheat. From the I-80 motorists' vantage point, north central Illinois is nothing but flat farmland. But, if they were to venture south a bit at the LaSalle/Utica exit, they would discover a wilderness that rivals some of our national parks in terms of sheer beauty and majesty.

How to get there:

Starved Rock State Park is a 7-mile long greenway of 2,630 acres along the river's south bank. The designated trails and other facilities for humans are in the eastern half of the park east of Route 178. Take I-80 west of Ottawa to the Utica/Route 178 exit. Head south three miles through Utica and across the Illinois River. The main entrance is to the left (east) .5 miles south of the river. For a more scenic, but slow route, take Route 71, which runs east and west south of I-80. First-time visitors should follow the signs either to the main parking area near the Visitor Center or to the lodge. Several other parking areas are shown on the map if you prefer parking closer to the trails farther east or at the campgrounds.

On my first visit, I parked near the DNR Visitor Center where I found a trail map and other brochures, learned about guided tours, and explored nature and historical exhibits. The Visitor Center is housed in a six-year old temporary trailer. Plans are to build a permanent and larger facility.

East of the main parking area is the trailhead that leads to Starved Rock, Lover's Leap, Eagle Cliff, and Beehive Overlooks, as well as French, Pontiac, and Wildcat Canyons. All are within a mile of the Visitor Center. Large trail maps at major intersections help guide you along the pathways.

Here, you can take wide, sandy pathways lined with fragile wildflowers through woodlands of red and white oaks, white pine, and cedar, and along clear streams. Close to the streams is a native shrub called witch hazel. This species actually blooms in late fall and winter, producing small yellowish-orange flowers that can be seen if you take the time to examine the shrub closely. Or try to learn the difference between white and red oaks. The white oaks have leaves with pointed lobes, the red oaks' leaves have rounded lobes.

Now is a good time to explain the trail designations you will find along the way. Colored dots are placed on trees or structures. Trails leading up to and on the bluffs are marked with B—brown dots or posts. Trails along the river are marked with R—red dots or posts. Interior canyon trails are designed I—with green dots or posts. Connecting trails are designated C also with green dots. Trails going

Starved Rock State Park (Western Section)

N

■ Major Stairways

P	(	✗	♦♦
Parking	Phone	Picnic	Restrooms

🐾	▲	♿	🎢
Fountain	Camping	Handicap Accessible	Playground

P ♦♦ ♿

Illinois Waterway
Visitor Center—
Open Seasonally

Boat Ramp

Illinois River

Starved Rock

Lover's Leap
Overlook

Plum Island

Dam

Eagle
Cliff
Overlook

Beehive
Overlook

P

P

Kickapoo
Canyon

Sac
Canyon

Aurora
Canyon

St.Louis
Canyon

P

French
Canyon

Wildcat
Canyon

Pontiac
Canyon

Lodge

(♦♦ 🐾

Visitor Center

Rt. 178

Rt. 71

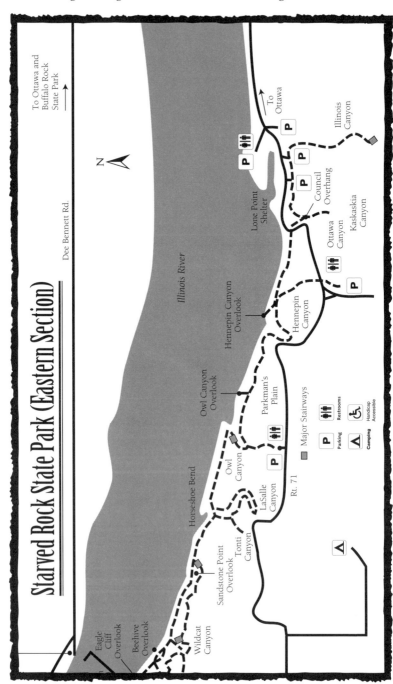

Starved Rock State Park (Eastern Section)

To Ottawa and Buffalo Rock State Park →

Dee Bennett Rd.

N

Illinois River

To Ottawa

Illinois Canyon

Lone Point Shelter

Council Overhang

Kaskaskia Canyon

Ottawa Canyon

Hennepin Canyon Overlook

Hennepin Canyon

Owl Canyon Overlook

Parkman's Plain

Horseshoe Bend

Owl Canyon

LaSalle Canyon

Rt. 71

Sandstone Point Overlook

Tonti Canyon

Wildcat Canyon

Eagle Cliff Overlook

Beehive Overlook

■ Major Stairways

P Parking

♿ Handicap Accessible

Restrooms

▲ Camping

away from the Visitor Center/Lodge are marked with yellow dots. Trails returning to the Visitor Center are marked with white dots. This can be a bit confusing at first, but is quite helpful once you get used to the designations.The Starved Rock trails are all for hiking only.

While the distance from the Visitor Center to the farthest east trail-Illinois Canyon is 4.7 miles, don't expect to be able to explore all the wonderful and challenging trails in one day. Trust me! The climbs up and down long stairs leading to the canyons and bluffs are tiring. Also some sections of the bluff trails are along steep drop-offs or through the canyon areas where caution and fresh legs are essential.

On my first visit I started with a climb up the long flight of stairs to Starved Rock, a 125-foot-high sandstone butte. At the top, I found a long circular wooden boardwalk with scenic views in all directions overlooking the Illinois River.

Humans settled here 10,000 years ago. First came the Hope-wellians, descendants of the hunter-gatherers, who migrated to the area after generations of roaming southeast from the land bridge that their ancestors crossed from Siberia to Alaska. Subsequently, Woodland and Mississippian cultures flourished in the Illinois River Valley, hunting and growing crops such as squash and sunflowers. In the 16th to 18th centuries, the Illiniwek populated the river valley. A tribe of approximately 6,000 people lived in a village along the river's north bank across from what is now the state park.

Father Marquette established a mission at the Native American village in 1675, two years after his explorations with Louis Jolliet. Later the French built Fort St. Louis on top of Starved Rock in 1683. In 1691 the fort was abandoned during the French and Indian wars. However traders and trappers sought refuge here until the fort burned around 1720.

The most infamous incident in the long history of Starved Rock occurred in the 1760s. Seeking revenge on the Illiniwek for the killing of Chief Pontiac, a war party of Ottawa surrounded a tribe of Illiniwek who had sought refuge on top of Starved Rock. According to legend, the siege ended with the starvation of all the trapped Illiniwek. Their sad tale lives on in the scenic beauty of this tall butte and the state park that surrounds it.

Looking east from the panoramic vista of Starved Rock is the Lover's Leap overlook, the second of seven sandstone buttes along the river trail. A short distance upriver is one of seven locks and dams that comprise the Illinois Waterway System. Built by the Army Corps of Engineers, the locks serve as a water stairway enabling barges and recreational crafts to pass from the Mississippi to Lake Michigan. An Illinois Waterway Visitor Center is located at the dam on the river's north bank. In winter, you can observe bald eagles feeding here. Sometimes the Army Corps sets up viewing scopes for the public. Down river (to the west) of Starved Rock, lies .8-mile long Plum Island.

South of Starved Rock, the trails form several overlapping loops leading up the bluffs to French, Pontiac, and Wildcat Canyons. I decided to follow the river trail heading east. Signs along the way warn the hiker to stay on the trails to help prevent erosion and dangerous drop-offs. In early May a sea of Virginia bluebells carpeted the forest floor along the trail as I approached Lover's Leap Overlook. The platform at the overlook offers a bench to rest and a wonderful view of Starved Rock to the west. The Eagle Cliff Overlook farther east offers the best view of the lock and dam.

The trail surface is sand most of the way with packed earth in some spots. If you are hiking with youngsters, keep them close at hand. The river trails often have steep drop-offs to the river, which has strong undertows at several locations. Similarly on the bluff and canyon trails, you will encounter very steep drop-offs. Take it slow. Watch your step, and enjoy the grandeur that surrounds you. Given the popularity and the relatively heavy use of the trails at Starved Rock, erosion is the biggest problem in the park particularly on the bluff trails. Over the past few years the DNR has constructed and continues to enhance an extensive system of wooden stairways, boardwalks, and railings for hiker safety and to help prevent erosion in the heavily used areas.

Farther east Beehive and Sandstone Point overlooks also offer picturesque views. At Sandstone Point Overlook, the river is .5 mile wide and quite shallow. On a windy day, high choppy waves create a feeling of a wild torrent across the waterway. Note the work of beavers along the river bank. At Horseshoe Bend, take the trail to the right which leads to peaceful Tonti and LaSalle Canyons. In the spring, the

Heritage Corridor Visitors Bureau

St. Louis Canyon in winter.

soothing sounds of the waterfalls welcome you. The LaSalle Canyon waterfall flows longer than most, usually into mid-summer.

Parking is available near the Owl Canyon Overlook 2 miles east of Route 178 and at several spots farther east near Ottawa and Illinois Canyons (see map). The eastern trails are much less used than those around the Visitors Center and lodge. Old bluff trails in the eastern section near Ottawa, Kaskasia, and Illinois canyons have been closed for safety reasons. Plans are to restore these trails over the next few years. Talk to the ranger at the Visitor Center to get current status.

West of the lodge you will find four more canyons. Take the pedestrian bridge over the auto road. An information signpost guides the trail user to the pathway right (north) to a stairway leading down to Aurora Canyon. The path to the left leads to an overlook of Sac Canyon. A multitude of ferns grow out from the canyon walls. A long boardwalk runs along the bluff. Near Route 178 is another trail intersection. The path right heads north to the boat ramp area on what is probably the least interesting trail in the park. The path left leads down to St. Louis Canyon. Spring-fed St. Louis Canyon has some waterfall if only a trickle during dry periods.

Enjoying all the trails and other items of interest at Starved Rock and nearby Matthiessen State Parks takes more than one day. You will find extensive camping facilities off of Route 71 and east of Route 178. Lodging and meals are available at Starved Rock Lodge and Conference Center south of the Visitors Center. Breakfast, lunch, and dinner are served every day. The historic lodge has 72 guest rooms and 18 cabins. An indoor swimming pool, sauna, and whirlpool help ease sore muscles after a long day on the trail. Interesting wood carvings and totem poles are spread throughout the grounds near the lodge. Several other campgrounds, bed and breakfasts, and cottage rental are available nearby. For example, Kishauwau on the Vermilion 5 miles south and one mile east of Starved Rock offers well-equipped country cottages with full kitchens and whirlpool tubs plus serene views of the beautiful Vermilion River. See the Appendix for telephone numbers and addresses for these and other lodging choices.

Call the DNR at 815-667-4726 for more information about Starved Rock State Park.

Matthiessen State Park

South of and adjoining Starved Rock State Park is a 1,938-acre wonderland where you can hike through a mile-long sandstone canyon in the northern section of the park called the Dells. A dell is a small narrow valley between hills, i.e., a ravine or canyon. Five miles of well-maintained hiking trails run along the ridges, through the canyon and near the river. Matthiessen shares much of the natural beauty to be found at Starved Rock but tends to be less frequently used and, therefore, a bit more peaceful.

How to get there:

Take Route 178 south of Utica, Starved Rock State Park, and Route 71 in LaSalle County. You will find two entrances along Route 178. The northern entrance leading to the Dells is 1 mile south of Route 71. The southern entrance to the Vermilion River Area is 1.7 miles south of Route 178.

The forests of Matthiessen, known to locals as Deer Park, are a good place to see spring wild-flowers such as hepatica, Jack-in-the-pulpit, and spring beauty. The Jack-in-the-pulpit provides beauty from spring through fall. In spring, three large, untoothed green leaves emerge from the forest floor. As the plant grows, a large leaf (pulpit) folds over the club-like blossoms (Jack) inside. Then, a dense cluster of green berries forms on the flower stalk. In late summer, the berries ripen into a brilliant red. Another well-known plant flourishes here, both as a vine, and a small ground plant, poison ivy. While the berries feed birds and other animals, the plant causes problems for us humans.

To access the hiking trails in the Dells Area, proceed past the equestrian parking to the main parking area at the end of the auto road near the large log fort. The fort is a replica of those built by the French in the late 17th and early 18th centuries. Next to the fort, you will find the trailhead. Walk down the long, wooden stairs to the bridge. Here Cascade Falls separates the Upper and Lower Dells. (See the map.) The trail marking system is identical to that of the one at Starved Rock described in Section 2. The Dells trail system consists of bluffs that encircle the canyon as well as two trails through the upper and lower sections of the long canyon. You will discover some splendid views on the bluffs overlooking the sandstone canyon walls. Take the wooden stairs down to the canyon floor. Concrete stepping stones help keep your feet dry particularly in spring or after a heavy rain when Matthiessen Lake overflows.

On a warm summer day the coolness of the canyon floor is refreshing. It is typically a serene, peaceful place. Cascade Falls at the northern end of the lower dells drops 45 feet. In spring or after a heavy rain, the waterfall is a sight to behold. Mother Nature's artwork can be found along the trails at other sites such as the Wishing Well, Strawberry Rock, and the Devil's Paint Box, sandstone sculptures created long ago by the fast, flowing waters.

The Lower Dell flows into the Vermilion River on its way north to the Illinois River. The bluff trail to the north leads to a bridge, dam, and overlook at Matthiessen Lake. The Lake Falls south of the lake is the beginning of the Upper Dell. Here again, long, wooden stairs lead down to the canyon floor. Hiking through the canyon you will see lush green ferns growing on the canyon walls. Nearby cliff swallows build nests in summer in niches in the sandstone walls. In fall, as you walk the canyon floor, you may hear the tea-kettle, tea-kettle, tea-kettle call of Carolina wrens. This delightful species prefers ravine and

Matthiessen State Park

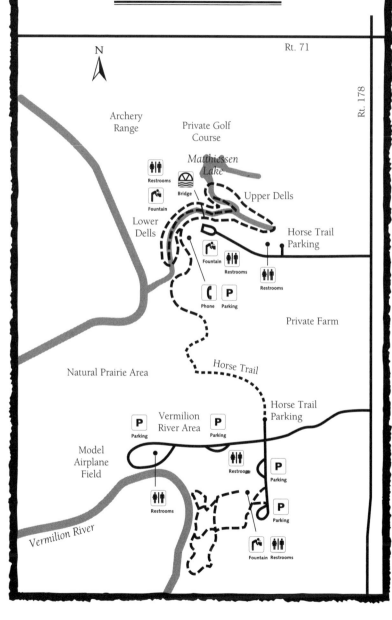

Matthiessen Lake.

canyon bottom habitats. Be sure to stay on the designated trails. There are steep cliffs along the trails with vertical drops of 80 feet or more.

A public phone, modern restrooms, water fountain, picnic tables, and a large shelter are available at the trailhead next to the fort. The nearby shelter, perched atop a ridge overlooking a woodland on the gradual descent to the canyon, is a good place for a break. If you are here in autumn, notice the abundance of hickory nuts scattered on the ground. Observe squirrels as they plant next year's hickory saplings. This sweet meat provides protein to the wild animals living here.

The bluff trail heading south below the fort leads to a 1-mile horse trail through an open meadow, which connects with the trail in the Vermilion River Area. (See map.) If you drive to the trailhead, the Vermilion River Area entrance road is .7 mile south of the Dells entrance. From the entrance road, take the first auto road south (left) and leave your vehicle in either of the two parking areas shown on the map. Note the information signposts at trail access points at both parking areas. Here you will find 1.9 miles of hiking trails on bluffs overlooking ravines and along the Vermilion River. There are lots of roots on the packed earth trails here so watch your step. The Department of Natural Resources is installing more information signposts and identifying items of interest along the trail. Installation of additional stairs in the Vermilion River Area and rock replenishment on the Dells Area trails will help to reduce erosion on the bluffs. The DNR prohibits the following activities at or near the trails at Matthiessen as well as Starved Rock State Parks:

• Rock or Ice-climbing
• Rappelling or Scrambling on Rocks
• Swimming or Wading
• Hiking Off of Marked Trails
• Metal Detecting
• Pets Not on a Leash
• Picking or Removing Anything
• Hiking After Dark
• Possessing Alcohol

These activities are hazardous to trail users and/or can cause erosion. Under certain conditions, ice-climbing is allowed at some sites in Starved Rock State Park. Call DNR at the number below for more information.

When the snows come, cross-country ski trails are open from December to March. Ski rental and trail maps are available at a trailer near the fort. The six miles of cross-country ski trails are identified by trail markers. In warmer weather, you can extend your hike by venturing onto the cross-country ski trails. However, portions of these trails become somewhat overgrown in summer and fall. You will also find separate equestrian trails here.

To make your visit more enjoyable I suggest you wear sturdy hiking boots and bring a compass. Also keep your youngsters close at hand. Pick up a trail brochure at the information signpost near the fort in the Dells Area or at Starved Rock State Park. The Vermilion River is also a popular place to canoe or raft. For more information call DNR at 815-667-4868.

Buffalo Rock and Illini State Parks

Two state parks in LaSalle County border the Illinois River and offer unique features as well as hiking trails with scenic river views.

Buffalo Rock State Park and the Effigy Tumuli

As you slowly climb the curvy and steep entrance road into Buffalo Rock State Park, you will pass tall limestone cliffs filled with ferns in the summer. Already this place feels different than most other parks. At the top, you will find 2.5 miles of trails. A .3-mile bluff trail offers scenic vistas overlooking the Illinois River to the south. (Also you can hike on a 2.2-mile trail that passes by a 770-foot-long catfish and a 2,070-foot-long snake.)

How to get there:

Take I-80 to the Ottawa (Route 23) exit. Head south into Ottawa. Turn right (west) on Route 6. Turn left on Boyce Memorial Drive and continue on past the I&M Canal State Trail access parking area. Turn right on Ottawa Avenue which becomes Dee Bennett Road. The park entrance is 2.7 miles west of Boyce Memorial Drive on the south side of the road. The Buffalo

A view from the limestone cliffs at Buffalo Rock State Park.

Rock I&M Canal State Trail access parking area is across the road.

The bluff trailhead is south of the first parking area. The path leads down a wooden stairway to a trail along a ridge overlooking the beautiful Illinois River. Two wooden platforms built into the limestone cliffs offer expansive views of the river.

After enjoying the river vistas, take the trail heading west along the river. At the first trail intersection, head right (north) to an overlook of the Effigy Tumuli. An effigy is a sculpted likeness or representation of an animal, person, or thing. Tumuli are burial mounds. In the 1940s, 250 acres of trees atop the limestone cliffs were cut down to get to a layer of coal. Strip mining polluted this land. Rain washed toxic sediments into the nearby river as well. In the 1980s, a partnership of individuals, organizations, and businesses devised a unique way to clean up the site. First the acidic soil was partially neutralized, then huge earthen sculptures were created as part of the regrading before reseeding. In the spirit of earthen mounds built long ago by Native Americans, enormous water creatures in the shape of a frog, a snake, a catfish, a turtle, and a water strider were created. To get the perspective of the entire work, an aerial view is needed, unless you are really tall!

CAUTION—there are steep drop-offs along the cliff edges. Stay on the designated trail throughout the tumuli area.

On my first visit, a weekday, the park was quiet and peaceful. I returned with my wife and son on a Sunday in late August. The continued rat-tat-tat of gunfire from the nearby gun club north of Dee Bennett Road made the area less peaceful.

Water, picnic tables, shelters, primitive camp sites, and restrooms are available at Buffalo Rock. The park office is open from 10 a.m. to 4 p.m. Call the DNR at 815-433-2224 for more information.

Illini State Park

The community of Marseilles lies on the northern bank of the Illinois River. Here the river, which contains a limestone riverbed and is especially shallow, drops three feet in 2 miles resulting in fast-moving rapids. It is a great place to enjoy the scenery but not so great for moving barges. The Army Corps of Engineers fixed the problem in the 1920s by constructing a canal along the river's south bank that bypassed the rapids and now is the Illinois River's main channel. Today, on a visit to the Illini State Park, you can stop by the Marseilles Lock and Dam at the far western end of the park. The lock is 600-feet-long, 110-feet-wide, and 42.5-feet-deep. Almost 12 million gallons of water are required to fill the lock each time a barge is raised or lowered.

How to get there:

Take 1-80 to the Marseilles exit. Head south on Main Street through downtown Marseilles. Cross over the Illinois River on a new auto bridge which includes a pedestrian walkway. The first left after you cross the river is the state park entrance road.

You'll find two short trails totaling 1.8 miles in the eastern section of this 510-acre park. The Marasottawa Trail is near Mallard Bay. A connector heads west to the Illini-Wek Cross-Country Ski Trail.

Extensive tent and trailer camping is available here. Shelters, restrooms, and water fountains are available throughout the park. A public phone is available at the park office at the entrance to the Great Falls campground. Call 815-795-2448 for more information.

Goose Lake Prairie State Natural Area

One hundred sixty some years ago, almost 60% of Illinois was a sea of tallgrass prairie. Buffalo, prairie chickens, and wolves roamed the area. Today 99% of that prairie is gone, replaced by shopping malls, factories, apartments, farmland, and my front yard. Over the past few years, interest in prairies and prairie restorations has increased. A 19,500-acre site, the Midewin National Tallgrass Prairie, is currently being restored in Will County. Meanwhile Romeoville, Lockport, West Chicago, Fermilab, Wolf Road, Churchill Woods, the Schulenburg Prairie at Morton Arboretum, the Chicago Botanic Garden, and other prairie restorations in northern Illinois have directly contributed to people's interest in and enjoyment of prairie forbs and grasses. But the big brother of all these beautiful prairies (pre-Midewin) is Goose Lake Prairie, a 2,537-acre state natural area in Grundy County east of Morris.

This is a bird-watcher's haven, especially in early summer when some rare birds including the state endangered Henslow's sparrow and the rapidly declining bobolink come to nest. Listen for the unusual calls of these birds when you visit. A Henslow's sparrow sings "flea-sick", while the bobolink sings a tinkling sound as it displays its white back and yellow nape.

How to get there:

Take Route 47 or I-55 south of the Illinois River to Pine Bluff-Lorenzo Road. Head west from I-55 or east from Route 47 to Jugtown Road. Head north on Jugtown to the Visitor Center parking area.

A 15-minute movie offered at the center is a good introduction to Goose Lake Prairie. In the film, you will learn that early settlers had a much greater appreciation for the woodland than for the prairie. The woodland provided logs for their homes, cooling shade in the summer, and shelter from the winter winds. The prairie, while having pretty flowers, offered only one use to the early settlers. That was the underlying fertile soil. John Deere's invention of the steel plow in 1837 gave farmers a way to turn over the thick prairie turf and grow high yielding corn and other crops. You can browse through exhibits describing different types of prairies as well as displays of plant and mammoth bone fossils. Climb the stairs inside the center to wooden observation decks that offer a good view of the surrounding prairie.

Goose Lake kept local settlers from farming the land here for most of the 19h century. In 1890, the lake was drained for planting. However, due to natural springs, the land remained too wet to plant and was used as pasture for livestock. Another attempt was made to drain the land 25 years later in 1915. You can see the drainage ditch along the trail. Again the drainage was unsuccessful and the land was considered useful only for grazing.

Seven miles of hiking and cross-country ski trails wind through Goose Lake Prairie east and south of the Visitor Center. Behind the center is the 1-mile Tall Grass Nature Trail. The trail surface is gravel and is wheelchair accessible. Get a trail guide brochure at the center which describes the effects of glaciers and the types of prairie grasses found here such as big bluestem and Indian grass.

Along the trail you will see a reconstruction of John and Agnes Cragg's cabin built nearby in the 1830s. The original cabin was on the Teamster Trail, the main route for cattle drivers taking their herds

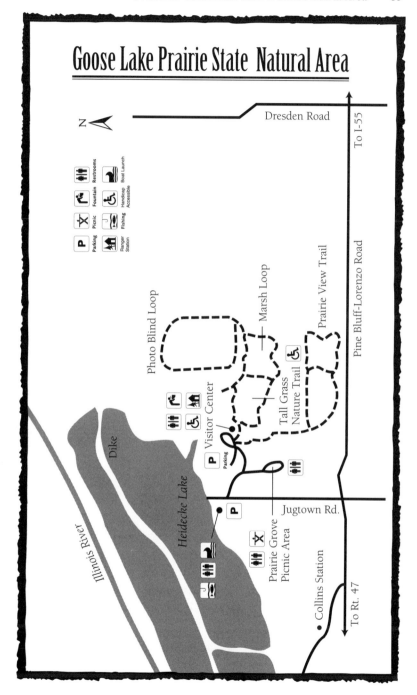

from Bloomington north to their final destination at the Chicago Stock Yards. The entrepreneurial Craggs provided overnight lodging for the teamsters housing as many as 30 each night. The Craggs added a second story to accommodate the six Cragg children. It was the only two-story home in Grundy County at the time. Locals called their home "The Palace". Note the size of the cabin. With eight family members and 30 teamsters as overnight guests, it gives claustrophobia a whole new meaning! Even with all our problems, I think I will stick to the present.

East of the interpretive trail is a .5-mile marsh trail. At the time of writing, part of the trail was closed. A short connector pathway leads by a replica of a conestoga wagon to the 2-mile Photo Loop Trail. On a warm August day, monarch butterflies flitted in the air near a small grove of hawthorn trees.

Except for the interpretive trail mentioned above, the rest of the pathways are mostly mowed turf. The terrain is essentially flat for the trails mentioned above. In the southern section, on the 3.5-mile Prairie View Trail, the terrain is a bit more rolling. Three large earthen

Hank Erdmann

Replica of the 1830's Craig cabin.

mounds in the southeastern section are the result of strip mining in the 1920s. An information signpost briefly describes efforts, with some success, to restore the strip-mined area by lowering the soil's acidity. Some prairie plants are beginning to grow again on this desolate land.

A short distance farther north on Jugtown Road and west of Goose Lake Prairie is 2,000-acre Heidecke State Fish and Wildlife Area. Commonwealth Edison (ComEd) owns and uses the large body of water as a cooling lake for the nearby Collins generating station. ComEd leases the lake to the DNR for fishing and hunting. A concessionaire rents boats and provides snacks and drinks in case you are hungry after your hike at Goose Lake Prairie.

A water fountain and restrooms are available inside the Goose Lake Visitor Center. A public telephone is in the parking area near the Prairie View Trailhead. Picnic areas with shelters, grills, and picnic tables are nearby. Visitor center hours are from 10 a.m. to 4 p.m. daily except for December-February when the site is closed on weekends. The DNR offers interpretive nature programs year-round. The trails are open for cross-country skiing when the snows come. Call 815-942-2899 for more information.

Kankakee River State Park

Nestled in the far southern reaches of Chicagoland, this 4,000-acre state park is an 11-mile greenway running along both banks of the Kankakee River. Limestone cliffs along the river and beautiful Rock Creek offer scenic views as well as a fine place for hiking and biking.

How to get there:

Accessible from either I-55 or I-57, the state park is near Bourbonnais six miles northwest of Kankakee and south of Joliet. Routes 102 and 113 parallel the park along the north and south banks of the river, respectively. The hiking and biking trails are all accessible from Route 102 along the river's east bank. The main park entrance is south of Warner Bridge Road.

At various times throughout the 17th, 18th, and 19th centuries, several tribes including the Chippewa, Kickapoo, Ottawa, and Potowatami hunted and fished along the river. French fur traders sought beaver pelts here. The French liked the area so much that many moved from Quebec to Bourbonnais in the late 1830s. After the I&M Canal opened in 1848, the Kankakee and Iroquois

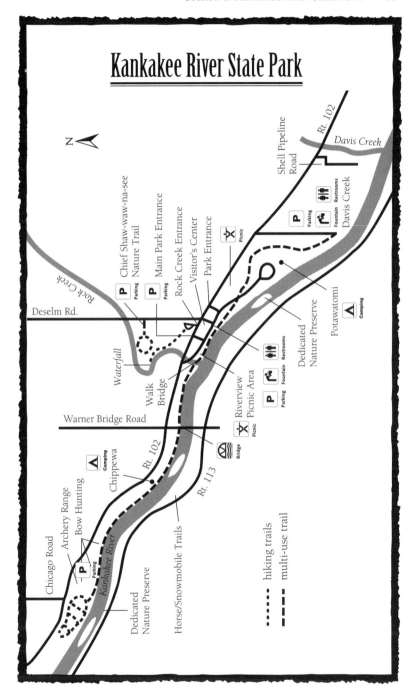

Kankakee River State Park

Navigation Company established a waterway route on the Kankakee from the canal southwest of Channahon to Warner's Landing near present day Warner Bridge Road.

A 10.5-mile bike trail runs north from near Davis Creek to the Area A parking lot near Chicago Road. The trail is easily accessible from five entrances along Route 102 (see map). I suggest first-timers take the main park entrance and stop at the nearby Visitors Center. Here you will find maps and brochures describing the trails and programs. Also you can see various displays such as an arrowhead collection as well as one on the identification of animal tracks. Coyotes, foxes, raccoons, squirrels, rabbits, opossums, deer, and other mammals live in this preserve. You can discover their presence, even when they have gone, by observing animal tracks. On snowy or muddy days, these creatures leave behind foot prints and other signs that they have been there. For example, a fox's tracks are straight and purposeful, unlike that of a domestic dog, which wanders from tree to tree. An opossum's foot prints show its opposable thumb. The print looks like a miniature human hand print. Signs of deer include turned over snow and mud where they have searched for acorns in winter and early spring.

In 1998, a 7.5-mile trail from Davis Creek to the Chippewa camping area was extended 3.5 miles to Chicago Road. The section from Davis Creek to the Potawatomi campground is a crushed limestone surface. The rest of the trail is asphalt surfaced. A good place to start the bike trail is south of the Visitors Center. Ample parking is available here. On my first visit, I headed southeast on the 10-foot-wide crushed limestone trail. Large pines and sugar maples line the trail overlooking the river. A bridge across a small stream leads into woodlands along both sides of the trail. The pathway is relatively flat except for a fairly steep downhill about 1.3 miles out. Large wooden markers show your progress every ½ mile. Soon you will notice narrow limestone paths heading off from the main trail. The numbered markers (#1–24) along the trail have a special use. The bike trail is closed for three weeks in November. During this period, the DNR sponsors a Physically Challenged Archery Hunt.

Watch out for washouts on the trail. In the areas most prone to washouts, the DNR installed concrete slabs to drain the water off the pathway. But since the trail runs through the river valley, there will always be an occasional washout.

The path runs north of the Potawatomi camping area and ends near the eastern boundary of the park at Davis Creek camping area (4.3 miles out). Davis Creek empties into the Kankakee a short distance south of here. A water fountain, shelter, picnic tables, and playground in a shaded oak grove make this a good spot for a rest. Walk your bike if you head down the narrow rock road to the riverside. You will need to backtrack to the Visitors Center to complete the trail. The round-trip back to the main entrance is 8.6 miles.

Heading northwest on the trail, note the Bert Steven's Memorial honoring the gentleman who was instrumental in establishing the park. The large, red granite stone was transported here from Canada during the last glacial period 12,000 years ago. North of the memorial is a large observation deck built over the river as well as is an older limestone overlook nearby. Both offer excellent views of the river and limestone cliffs along the southern bank of the Kankakee.

Winding its way along the river, the trail soon leads to the River View Picnic Area. Breakfast, lunch, and dinner are served at the concession building here year-round (10.3 miles out). Bicycle and canoe rentals are also available. Call 815-932-3337 for more information.

A long suspension bridge transports bicyclists and hikers over beautiful Rock Creek Canyon. The stone-filled stream reminds me of the Great Smoky Mountain National Park (without the mountains). This is the same Rock Creek that flows through Monee Reservoir and Raccoon Grove Nature Preserve 18 miles to the northeast (see Section 15).

Northwest of Rock Creek Canyon, the trail runs through woodlands with a steep downhill leading through an underpass of Warner Bridge Road to the Chippewa Campground. On my first visit, the asphalt surface before the underpass had deteriorated. A trail improvement project in 1998 eliminated that problem and extended the trail 3.5 miles. The trail ends in the Area A parking lot 10.5 miles out. Returning to the main entrance area where we started makes for a 21-mile round-trip.

North of Route 102 are two hiking trails along or near Rock Creek.

One path leads to a beautiful waterfall. The trailhead for the 1.5-mile Rock Creek Trail is in the Rock Creek Day Use Area. Take the auto road a short distance east of the main entrance. You will find a trail sign at the second parking area off the auto road. Follow the brown trail markers along an old asphalt road north. Unfortunately the creek with its beautiful sandstone cliffs is not easily visible from the trail. However you will know when you are approaching the waterfall when you hear the sounds of rushing water. Be very careful getting a closer look. There are no established trails out to the waterfall, only narrow footpaths with steep drop-offs into the canyon.

Parking and the trailhead for the second hiking trail are located on Deselm Road .3 mile east of the main office. The parking lot is .8 mile north on Deselm Road just past the Riding Stables.

The Chief Shaw-waw-nas-see Nature Trail is a 1.5-mile self-guided nature walk on a footpath along Rock Creek. There are 20 numbered stations which correspond with a brochure that is available at the Visitors Center. One of the stations is a boulder marking Chief Shaw-waw-nas-see's gravesite. Following the Blackhawk War of 1832, the

Stacey Powers, Illinois Department of Natural Resources

Kankakee River State Park waterfall.

Potowatami ceded their land here to the U. S. Government. Most left the area, although the chief refused to leave his "Kankakee", the Potowatami word for wonderful land.

When the snows come, a 12-mile linear cross-country ski trail runs along the river ending in the northwestern section of the park. A 4-mile section of the cross-country ski trail in the northwestern section of the park is also open for hiking through oak woodlands and prairie. Follow the cross-country ski trail signs north from the Chippewa Camping Area. The pathway through the prairie is infrequently mowed and can be overgrown in the summer. I saw two wild turkeys off in the distance on an early spring hike. The secluded loop trail is north of an archery range and bow-hunting area. Park in Area A in October and November during the bow-hunting season. Check with the park office during fall and winter to determine the sections closed during hunting season.

The DNR offers nature programs and guided hikes year-round. The state park is also a popular fishing and canoeing spot. Swimming is not allowed due to the strong currents and steep drop-offs common in both the Kankakee River and Rock Creek. Water, restrooms, picnic tables, and shelters are available throughout the park. You will find public phones at the Visitors Center and the concession store. The park closes at 10 p.m.

Extensive tent and RV camping facilities are also available here. A 15-mile equestrian and snowmobile trail runs along the southern bank near Route 113. In season, areas of the park are open for hunting along Route 113. Call the DNR at 815-933-1383 for more information.

Midewin National Tallgrass Prairie

Dolomite prairie, one of the rarest natural communities in North America, exists right here in Will County at the Midewin National Tallgrass Prairie. Incorporating more than 19,500 acres, Midewin also includes grasslands, savanna, wetlands, seeps, upland forests, and three streams. These landscapes today provide habitat for 348 species of native plants, 108 species of breeding birds, 40 aquatic species, 23 species of reptiles and amphibians, 25 insect species that require native plant communities to survive, and 27 species of wild mammals. Midewin provides home to 16 or more endangered and threatened species, including the loggerhead shrike. It also harbors Illinois' largest breeding population of upland sandpipers, a state-endangered species.

This national treasure exists because of a 1996 federal law establishing the site as the nation's first federally designated tallgrass prairie. The legislation designated the transfer of a 19,165 acre parcel of land in Illinois from the U. S. Army to the U. S. Department of Agriculture Forest Service, and mandates that Midewin be managed to meld four primary objectives:

• To conserve, restore, and enhance the native populations and habitats of fish, wildlife, and plants.

• To provide opportunities for scientific, environmental, and land use education and research.

• To allow the continuation of existing agricultural uses of lands within Midewin National Tallgrass Prairie for the next 20 years, or for compatible resource management uses thereafter.

• To provide recreational opportunities that are not inconsistent with the above purposes.

The land is here because some 23,500 acres in this area once contained the Joliet Arsenal where 14,000 men and women once worked to make and store explosives to help win World War II. Later, the arsenal provided munitions during the Korean and Vietnam conflicts. By the late 1970s, the arsenal was closed and the land was leased to local farmers. Now it has been deeded to the nation's people.

How to get there:

Take I-55 south of Joliet and northwest of Kankakee to the Wilmington exit (#241). Head east 4 miles past the Des Plaines Wildlife Conservation Area to Route 53. Turn left (north) and proceed 1 mile to Midewin headquarters.

"Midewin" is an Algonquin word referring to the "healing society", very appropriate given the plans to restore grassland habitats on such a massive scale. Midewin will be the largest prairie east of the Mississippi River. Nearby are other large natural areas, the Des Plaines Wildlife Conservation Area, Goose Lake Prairie State Natural Area, the Illinois and Michigan Canal, and McKinley Woods Forest Preserve. Also close by to the west is the confluence of the Des Plaines, Kankakee, and DuPage Rivers that merge to form the Illinois River.

Ecologists say this site is important because it links 40,000 acres of prairies, wetlands, woodlands, and rivers. Large natural areas provide habitat for specific animals requiring huge acreage in which to nest. In addition, the large acreage can host a great diversity of plants and animals. Living on the preserve right now are two unusual grassland species that you might observe on a visit, the loggerhead shrike and the upland sandpiper. The shrike is a cunning predator that swoops on its prey, a mouse, perhaps, then impales it on the thorns of a tree, where the food hangs like a sausage until meal time. You may also hear the unusual "wolf-whistle" call of the state-endangered upland sandpiper. Standing in the grasslands watching the male give its lovely, aerial courtship display, makes you imagine you have retreated to a time when this land was once a huge, untouched expansive prairie.

The U. S. Forest Service, the Illinois DNR, the Forest Preserve District of Will County, and other agencies along with volunteers are working to restore this area so that the sandpipers and other species can remain, while species that once lived here might return. In fact, scientists plan to reintroduce bison and elk to the area. Grazing bison helped keep some of the grasses short, which in turn provided nest sites for Henslow's sparrows and other species.

A volunteer group, the Midewin Tallgrass Prairie Alliance, along with volunteers from other organizations help scientists in their job. These people have already planted 22 acres of seed beds to grow prairie forbs and grasses.

A major part of the restoration work will involve removing the heavy metals and other toxins used in manufacturing munitions. As this work is completed, Midewin will become a major hiking and biking mecca. The Joliet Arsenal contained 166 miles of railroad track and 220 miles of road, some of which can potentially be converted into hiking and biking paths. A 10-mile rails-to-trails conversion is planned on the right-of-way of the old Chicago, Milwaukee, and St. Paul Railroad line that runs from Manhattan north to Joliet. This new trail will connect Midewin with the NHC trails, the Chicago greenway trail system, the Grand Illinois Trail, and the American Discovery Trail. See Section 23.

Though public access is limited to Midewin at this writing, you may call the Midewin headquarters at 815-423-6370 for the latest information.

Joliet Trails

The largest municipality in Will County is Joliet with a population of 90,000. Often known today for its two riverboat casinos and Joliet State Correctional Center, this city has a long history as a prominent industrial town and is known as the City of Steel and Stone. In the 19th century, more than 50 quarries were opened between Lemont and Joliet to mine dolomite, also called Joliet limestone. The walls of the I&M Canal in Lemont and Lockport are lined with dolomite. Today the remaining quarries produce crushed stone for many uses including trail surfaces for the I&M Canal State Trail.

Joliet Iron Works Historic Site

In the 1850s, the furnaces at Joliet Iron Works began producing iron rails to meet the demands of the rapidly expanding railroad lines. The plant was located along the I&M Canal to provide waterway transportation for the incoming iron ore and for the outgoing finished iron rails. A few years later, a new technology using Bessemer converters provided the means to produce more durable steel rails.

In the first decade of the 20th Century, new ovens were added to produce coke for iron smelting. At the time, the Joliet Iron Works was one of the most efficient steel producers in the country, employing close to 5,000 workers. However, during the Depression of the 1930s, demand for steel plummeted. The Joliet Iron Works was shut down. The smoke stacks were removed and most of the large industrial site, once a beehive of activity, has remained dormant until recently. Now you can hike and bike through the site along the I&M Canal and near the Des Plaines River.

How to get there:

On bicycle from the north take the Gaylord Donnelley Canal Trail through Lockport (see Section 10). From the south, take the I&M Canal State Trail to Brandon Road Lock and Dam and follow the NHC designated on-street bike route through Joliet described below. By motor vehicle, take Route 53 into downtown Joliet. Take Route 53/Scott Street north of Route 30 to Columbia Street. Turn right. You will find a large parking area here.

Following the designation of the I&M Canal National Heritage Corridor, the Lockport Township Park District, the Forest Preserve District of Will County, and the Illinois Department of Natural Resources jointly established 260-acre Heritage Park along the I&M Canal. The Joliet Iron Works Historic Site is located in the southern section of Heritage Park.

This is unlike any park I have ever seen. Here you will find foundations from old buildings and ruins remaining from the blast furnaces, stoves, limestone quarry ponds, underground tunnels, and slag piles. At the time of writing, two trails were under construction here, a 2.7-mile crushed limestone Heritage Trail along the I&M Canal and a 1-mile concrete hiking-only path through the ruins with interpretive signposts along the way. The multi-use Heritage Trail and the on-street bike route described below are both part of the 88-mile backbone NHC trail route mentioned in the introduction.

Joliet On-Road Bike Route

In 1998, a 3-mile designated on-street bike tour route will be

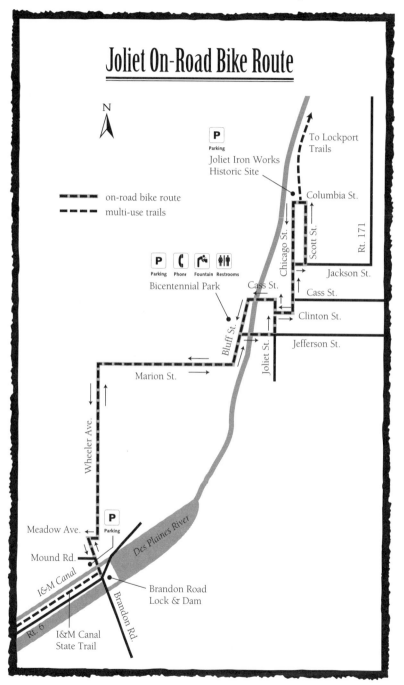

Joliet On-Road Bike Route

N

P Parking
Joliet Iron Works
Historic Site

- - - - on-road bike route
- - - - multi-use trails

To Lockport
Trails

Columbia St.

Chicago St.

Scott St.

Rt. 171

Jackson St.

P Parking **☎** Phone **⛲** Fountain **🚻** Restrooms
Bicentennial Park

Cass St.

Cass St.

Clinton St.

Bluff St.

Joliet St.

Jefferson St.

Marion St.

Wheeler Ave.

Des Plaines River

P Parking

Meadow Ave.

Mound Rd.

I&M Canal

Brandon Road
Lock & Dam

Brandon Rd.

Rt. 6

I&M Canal
State Trail

established in Joliet along or near the Des Plaines River. From the
north the bike route will start at the southern terminus of the Joliet
Iron Works trail at Columbia and Scott Streets. The map on page 73
shows the route. Trail banners will help the cyclist stay on course.
Along the bike route, you will find markers pointing out historic sites
and nearby points of interest such as historic churches and mansions,
Rialto Square Theatre, Joliet Union Station, and Bicentennial Park.
The on-road route will end at a parking lot at Mound Road west of
Brandon Road. Here you will find the new northern trailhead for the
61-mile I&M Canal State Trail (see Section 1).

Will-Joliet Bicentennial Park

Bicentennial Park at 201 Jefferson Street in downtown Joliet is one
of the many National Heritage Corridor visitor centers. Here you can
take a short walk along the bluffs overlooking the Des Plaines. Plaques
spread throughout the grounds and inside the park theatre lobby
provide information about downtown Joliet's early days. James McKee
built and operated a mill and dam here beginning in 1834. With the
opening of the I&M Canal in 1848, McKee's business folded but
commerce in the community of Joliet flourished. An attractive brick
Riverwalk extends two blocks from Cass Street (Western Avenue) to
Jefferson Street on the west side of the Des Plaines River. Lovely
murals along Jefferson Street and the cliffs of Bicentennial Park paint
a picture story of the city's history. Check out the beautiful in-ground
mosaic depicting downtown Joliet next to the police station across
Jefferson. Bicentennial Park will be a good place to park if you plan to
head north or south on the NHC trails. Here you'll find water, benches, restrooms and a public phone in the theatre lobby. An outdoor
band shell is a popular spot for summer concerts.

How to get there:

Of course, the best way is via bike from the on-road bike route
described above. By motorized vehicle, take I-80 or Routes 30, 52, or
53 into downtown Joliet. Bicentennial Park is on Jefferson at historic
Bluff Street on the west bank of the Des Plaines River. From the east
take Route 30/Cass Street which becomes Western Avenue after you

cross the river. From the west take Jefferson Street to Bicentennial Park. (See map.)

A 6-block walking tour of historic downtown has recently been established. Bicentennial Park and the nearby murals are part of a Center City Mural and Architecture Walking Tour through downtown Joliet. Pick up a brochure at Bicentennial Park. Call 1-800-926-CANAL for more information.

As well as becoming a major segment of the NHC trail system, in a few years, the western trailhead for the Old Plank Road Trail will be extended to Washington Street in downtown Joliet. A section of the trail in Joliet will run on an abandoned elevated railway right-of-way. See Section 9 for more on the Old Plank Road Trail.

Pilcher Park

In spring wildflowers welcome you to the maple/oak forest at Pilcher Park. Eighty years ago this land was a private arboretum. In 1921, Robert Pilcher donated 327 acres of virgin woodland and gardens to the City of Joliet. Today you can hike and bike the trails, golf at nearby Woodruff Golf Course, or fish in Hickory Creek. Over the past few decades the park has been expanded to 630 acres including Higinbotham Woods to the west. You will find 2 miles of hiking paths and 3 miles of trail open for bicycling.

How to get there:

Take U.S. Route 30 (Cass Street) east of downtown Joliet. The entrance is .3 mile east of the intersection of Briggs Street and Route 30. Turn left into the park. Continue straight past the statue of Robert Pilcher. Hickory Creek is to the right. The next road to the left leads to Pilcher Park Nature Center. You will find a parking area in front of the attractive pine log Nature Center. A large, colorful totem pole built in 1912 greets you at the entrance.

Inside the center, you will find a turtle pond, several aquariums with catfish, sturgeon, bass, sunfish, crappie, and perch as well as a bird viewing area.

Most of the trails run through hardwood forest. There are three types of trails here: hiking, asphalt multi-use, and gravel multi-use.

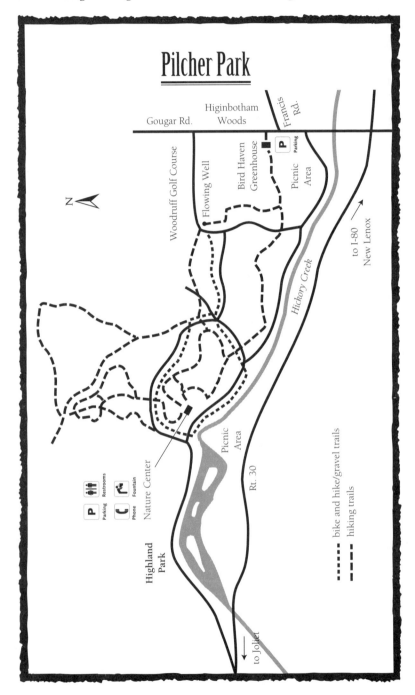

Pilcher Park

Higinbotham Woods

Gougar Rd.

Francis Rd.

Woodruff Golf Course

Flowing Well

Bird Haven Greenhouse

P Parking

Picnic Area

to I-80 New Lenox

Hickory Creek

N

Picnic Area

Rt. 30

Nature Center

P Parking

Restrooms

Phone

Fountain

Highland Park

bike and hike/gravel trails

hiking trails

to Joliet

Access to hiking trails (the Trail of Oaks, the Sensory Trail, as well as trails to the Bird Haven Greenhouse & Conservancy and the Flowing Well) can be found behind the Nature Center. The hiking trails, which mostly run north and east of the nature center building, are a mixture of woodchip and packed earth surface ranging from 2-to-6-feet wide. Small wooden boardwalks throughout the park help keep your shoes dry in the spring. Along the path on the Trail of the Oaks, you will see a 270-year-old bur oak, the largest tree in the park. There is also a short hiking trail along Hickory Creek east of the Nature Center.

The multi-use trails are mostly north of the Nature Center and can be accessed via an auto road or the gravel trail that loops around the nature center. This area of the park is quiet and serene. An old and narrow asphalt road loops through the northern section of the park. Long closed to auto traffic, the trail surface has sections of deteriorating asphalt, loose gravel, cracks, and tree branches on the trail. I recommend either a mountain or hybrid bike. The gravel trails consist of a loop around the Nature Center and a spur east to the Flowing Well. Here you can drink natural spring mineral water that flows constantly from the artesian well. The gravel trails are open for bicycles; however, there are some sections with large gravel, not conducive for a stable bike ride if you are on a road bike.

You can also access the Pilcher Park trails from the Bird Haven Greenhouse and Conservatory.

How to get there:

Take Gougar Road north of Route 30. Entrance is .5 mile north of the intersection of Gougar and Route 30. Turn left into the parking area.

After walking the trails, you can wander through the greenhouse's beautiful array of plants including a tropical house and cacti room. Outdoor gardens are open from June through October. At the time of writing, a large Horticultural Center was under construction adjacent to the greenhouse. Call 815-741-7278 for more information.

Trails in Pilcher Park are open for cross-country skiing when the snows come. Water, restrooms, and a bike rack are available at the Nature Center. Programs, some overnight, are offered throughout the

Joliet Park District

Pilcher Park Nature Center.

year. Nature Center hours are daily 9 a.m. to 6 p.m. March through October and 9 a.m. to 4:30 p.m. November through February. Call 815-741-7277 for more information.

Higinbotham Woods

East of Pilcher Park is Higinbotham Woods. Ruins of earthworks constructed by early Native Americans and/or the French are scattered throughout the woods.

How to get there:

Take Gougar Road north of Route 30 and east of Pilcher Park to Francis Road. Head east .6 mile. The parking area is to the left. You will see a large boulder here, carried by a glacier 12,000 years ago. The boulder serves as a monument with inscriptions describing a French fort built in 1730, a trading post built in 1829, as well as sad tales from early Indian/French battles, and the Blackhawk War of 1829. A short packed earth trail (.2 mile) heads north along a ridge overlooking a ravine to the site of the alleged old French fort.

Old Plank Road Trail

In the mid-1800s, early settlers in northern Illinois had the arduous task of moving wagons loaded with corn, wheat, and household goods on dirt roads that connected rapidly growing communities and farms. With spring thaws and rains, the dirt roads became murky mire. One solution was to cover the dirt road with planks of wood laid side-by-side that provided a drier more stable surface. By the 1880s, the plank roads were mostly gone, sometimes replaced by more efficient railway lines.

In the late 1970s, the Forest Preserve District of Will County and many other agencies such as Rich Township, the Illinois Department of Natural Resources, the Open Lands Project, and the communities of Frankfort, Matteson, and Park Forest became interested in preserving a 20-mile greenway on the right-of-way of an abandoned Penn Central rail line. The goal was to establish an east-west trail through the wetlands, woodlands, and communities of Cook and Will Counties from Joliet east to Park Forest. After many years of planning and consensus-building, a 13.1-mile section of the trail was opened in the summer of 1997 running from Hickory Creek Preserve northwest of Frankfort in Will County east to Western Avenue in Park Forest in Cook County.

How to get there:

You will find numerous places to park in the communities along the way. Here we will describe three locations. The western trailhead is currently located in the Hickory Creek Preserve in Mokena. Take Lincoln Highway (Route 30) west of Route 45 or east of Schoolhouse Road to the Hickory Creek Junction entrance. Here a .5-mile connector trail heads south starting with a 120-foot-long pedestrian bridge across Route 30. Another good place to park is in nearby downtown Frankfort. Take Route 45 south of Route 30 to White Street. Proceed south .5 mile on White to Kansas Street. Parking is available to the right next to the village green, which is adjacent to the trail. There is currently no designated parking at the eastern trailhead at Western Avenue. A good place to park on the east side is at Logan Park in Park Forest west of Orchard Drive and south of Route 30.

The trail is a 10-foot-wide asphalt surface with 3-foot-wide shoulders. Take it easy if you are on your bike. You will encounter hikers, rollerbladers, and young children in carriages along the way. Go slowly and enjoy the beautiful wetlands, prairies, and woodlands. Many trail bridges, underpasses and push-to-walk stoplights offer easy crossing of the busiest highways, railroad tracks, and some creeks. In addition, you will find approximately 15 road/street crossings along the trail without stoplights. Obey the stop signs at each road crossing. Patrolling community police ticket violators. The trail is open from dawn to dusk.

Let's take the 13.1-mile trip from Hickory Creek Junction to Park Forest. Using my finely honed mathematic skills, I calculated a 26.2-mile round-trip. Currently there are only a few sites with easy access to water and restrooms on the trail. So take advantage of the facilities at a second and larger parking area north of the trailhead at Hickory Creek Junction before heading out. After crossing the trail bridge over Route 30, the path heads south near an attractive residential neighborhood before curving east at .5 miles out. After a couple of street crossings, you will pass by Michele Bingham Memorial Park and then

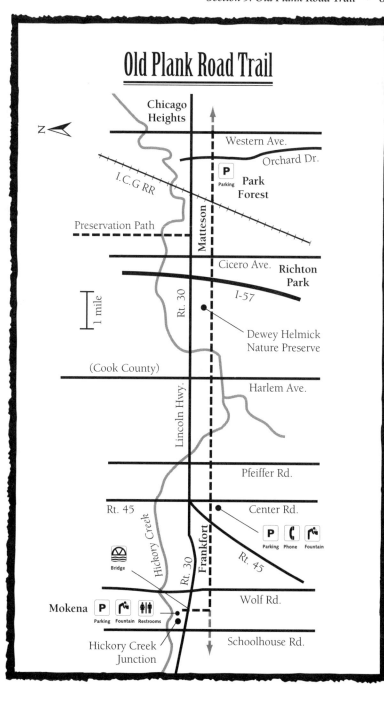

Old Plank Road Trail

N

Chicago Heights

Western Ave.

Orchard Dr.

P Parking **Park Forest**

I.C.G RR

Matteson

Preservation Path

Cicero Ave. **Richton Park**

I-57

Rt. 30

1 mile

Dewey Helmick Nature Preserve

(Cook County)

Lincoln Hwy.

Harlem Ave.

Pfeiffer Rd.

Rt. 45

Center Rd.

Hickory Creek

Frankfort

P Parking C Phone 🚰 Fountain

Rt. 45

Bridge

Rt. 30

Mokena P Parking 🚰 Fountain 🚻 Restrooms

Wolf Rd.

Hickory Creek Junction

Schoolhouse Rd.

Old Plank Road Trail in Frankfort.

cross over another long trail bridge at Route 45 as you enter Frankfort.

At 3.4 miles out you will come to Oak Street in Frankfort's picturesque historic district. A bike rack and benches are available in the manicured village green if you want to explore the nicely restored shops. Food and drink are available at a deli next to the trail and several other nearby restaurants. A bike shop is near the deli. A former grainery towers over the nearby buildings.

Continuing east, you will pass through more new home developments along the trail. Near the Pfeiffer Road crossing, the housing developments give way to cornfields. Wooden mile markers along the trail help you keep track of your progress. You will also see a few old stone markers, remnants of the railroad days.

At 5.2 miles out, a bridge crosses over Hickory Creek. Here the trail runs on a narrow high ridge. Farther east a beautiful woodland embraces the pathway through Hunters Woods Forest Preserve. You will enter Cook County at Harlem Avenue (6.6 miles out). South of the trail is an Illinois Nature Preserve that protects an extensive prairie and wetland from future development. The Dewey Helmick Nature Preserve in Rich Township and the Plank Road Nature Preserve surround the trail. Over 100 different species of prairies forbs and grasses exist in these nature preserves. Beginning in spring and continuing through late fall, a succession of prairie forbs and grasses grow and bloom. First come the spiderworts with their deep blue flowers. Then come blazing stars, with fuzzy purplish pink flowers that bloom from the top down, an unusual occurrence in the plant world. Some people call them gay feathers. Complementing the purple hue of the blazing stars are the yellow flowers of the compass plant and prairie dock. The prairie dock's large leaves hug the ground, while the compass plant's toothed, deeply lobed leaves grow higher on the plant, leaning toward the sun. In late summer, various goldenrods and asters take their place in the prairie menagerie. You will return to civilization with an I-57 underpass west of Matteson at 9.2 miles out.

The path continues east past a large strip mall at Cicero Avenue (Route 50). Lincoln Mall is north of the trail. Use the push-to-walk pedestrian button to cross Cicero at the stoplight (9.7 miles out). Soon you will come to a trail intersection. Preservation Path is a 1.4-mile asphalt trail that heads north (left) to Route 30 in Matteson. This path will be extended to connect with the southern section of Cook County Forest Preserve District's Tinley Creek Trail.

After an overpass of Governors Highway, the path leads to Main

Street in Matteson. Here you will pass by Caboose Park and a Metra parking area followed by an underpass of the railroad tracks (11.5 miles out). Logan Park in Park Forest (12.5 miles out) is soon followed by an overpass of Orchard Drive and the trail's temporary end at Western Avenue (13.1 miles out).

Plans are to extend the trail 8 miles west through New Lenox and on to Washington Street in Joliet. The first addition, 3.3 miles of trail from Hickory Creek Junction to Lions Park in New Lenox, is scheduled for completion in 1998. The remaining 4.7 miles, from New Lenox to Washington Street in Joliet, is planned for completion in a few years. The Old Plank Road Trail will connect with a designated on-road bike route through Joliet (see Section 8), which is part of the National Heritage Corridor backbone trail system heading south to the 61-mile I&M Canal State Trail and north to the 2.7-mile Joliet Iron Works Trail. Also an extension east to the Cook County Forest Preserve District's Thorn Creek Bicycle Trail addition in Chicago Heights is planned.

As well as offering Chicagoland trail users a peaceful place to hike and bike along some beautiful natural areas, the Old Plank Road Trail is part of a much bigger picture under development. The trail is a significant link in the 500+ mile Grand Illinois Trail that loops through northern Illinois. In addition, the Old Plank Road Trail is also part of the 6,300-mile American Discovery Trail that will extend from the Atlantic to the Pacific Ocean. As you travel the Old Plank Road Trail, watch for markers identifying the Grand Illinois and the American Discovery Trail. (See Section 23 for a brief description of both the Grand Illinois and the American Discovery Trails.)

Since opening in 1997, the Old Plank Road Trail has been well received by trail users. A large part of the funding for the trail came from the federal Intermodal Surface Transportation and Efficiency Act, affectionately known as ISTEA, which provides funds for new trails and bike paths as well as highways. Trails provide local residents with a non-automotive means of getting to parks, libraries, schools, train commuter stations, stores, and churches. The Old Plank Road is meeting both its reasons for being, recreation and an alternative, non-motorized means of transportation.

Lockport Trails

The heart and soul of the NHC is in Lockport where field headquarters for the canal construction were located. In downtown Lockport you will find the elegantly restored Gaylord Building, which, of course, was built with locally mined dolomite limestone. Today it is owned by the National Trust for Historic Preservation. At this I&M Canal Visitor Center, you will find History Galleries featuring hands-on activities. The Gaylord Building is also home to the Lockport Gallery of the Illinois State Museum, and the award-winning Public Landing Restaurant. Nearby are the I&M Canal Museum and a restored Pioneer Settlement.

How to get there:

Take Route 53 south of I-55 or north of Joliet to Route 7. Head east on Route 7/9th Street across the high-level bridge which passes over the Des Plaines River, the Chicago Sanitary and Ship Canal, and Deep Run Creek. After crossing Canal Street and just before the railroad tracks, turn right into a city parking lot across from the Pioneer Settlement.

Here you can access the 2.5-mile Gaylord Donnelley Canal Trail that runs north and south along the bank of the old canal.

Before or after you hike or bike the trail, visit the historic Gaylord Building. Take the underpass (beneath Route 7/9th Street) north past the Pioneer Settlement. Part of the building was completed in 1838 to store canal construction equipment. At the Visitor Center, you can discover the part the I&M Canal played in the development of northeastern Illinois. Be sure to see the excellent 10-minute video as well as other canal-related exhibits. Hours are from 10 a.m. to 5 p.m. Tuesday through Sunday.

Nearby is the Will County Historical Society's Pioneer Settlement. As you wander through the village of original buildings from around Will County, you will find a one-room school, blacksmith shop, jail, and several other structures. Trail users who do not follow the Rules of the Trail on page 21 are held overnight in the old jail! You'll find a bike rack and water fountain along the canal near the Pioneer Settlement.

One block east at 803 South State Street is the I&M Canal Museum located in the old Canal Commission Headquarters built in 1837. Preserved by the Will County Historical Society, the museum is filled with pictures, artifacts, tools, and other 19th century memorabilia. Hours are 1 to 4:30 p.m. daily.

North of the Gaylord Building, the path runs through a parking area behind some businesses. The asphalt trail heads .5 mile north past the site of the original canal boat yard of the 1840's. The trail, tree-lined and well-maintained, ends at 2nd Street. Here it will connect with the 20-mile Centennial Trail under development at the time of writing (see Section 11). Until the Centennial Trail is completed, you will have to backtrack to the parking lot.

Continue south of 9th Street along the canal. You will pass by the limestone Norton Building. Once a cereal manufacturing plant, now it is all that is left of a large complex that once included a Hydraulic Basin, where early settlers built a flour mill, grain elevator, and sawmill to take advantage of the energy derived from flowing water. The trail leads to Lock #1 near Division Street. This is the first of a series of 15 locks that were built on the I&M Canal. The drop from

Heritage Corridor Visitors Bureau

Gaylord Building in Lockport.

the Chicago River to the Illinois River at LaSalle/Peru is 141 feet.
Therefore, barges or packets headed east had to be gradually raised,
and boats headed west lowered. Initially large wooden gates were
manually opened and closed. An information signpost at the lock
describes in more detail how this procedure worked.

A modern dam and lock south of Lockport on the Chicago Sanitary
and Ship Canal is part of the present-day Illinois Waterway System,
which carries on the tradition and the work of raising and lowering
the water level for transport barges, pleasure boats, and other water-
craft traveling between Chicago and the Mississippi River.

The trail continues south of Division and left of the I&M Canal.
Head south for another mile to Dellwood Park and Fraction Run
Creek. Here the trail is crushed limestone. If you are headed to
Dellwood Park, walk your bike across the railroad tracks and past
the narrow trail along the cliff. Note the Interpretive sign that briefly
describes the history of Dellwood Park. The wooden platform to the
left leads along Fraction Run Creek to Dellwood Park. The main NHC
backbone trail system continues southwest of the railroad tracks. Here

the Lockport trail connects with the Heritage Trail (See Section 8.)

Dellwood Park

Dellwood Park was quite an amusement attraction in the early 20th century. The Chicago & Joliet Electric Railway Company built the park in 1906 to increase the number of railway riders.

A boathouse, dance hall, grandstand for races, merry-go-round, open air theatre, restaurant, and other attractions made this a popular spot for thousands of annual visitors from Chicago until a major fire destroyed many of the buildings in 1930.

Today Dellwood Park lives on as a community park. Here you will find 2 miles of asphalt and crushed gravel pathways as well as a performing arts center, picnic pavilions, playgrounds, and ballfields.

How to get there:

Hiking or biking via the Gaylord Donnelley Canal Trail or the Heritage Trail is the best way. If you have a motorized vehicle, take State Street/Route 171 south of 9th Street in Lockport. Turn left at Parkview Lane.

A 1-mile asphalt trail loops around the ballfields. Another 1 mile of gravel and crushed limestone trail runs up and down the hills and ravines near Fraction Creek. Be very careful on the gravel trails. Walk your bike down the steep hills. Water, shelters, picnic tables, and restrooms are available in Dellwood Park.

The community celebrates its heritage with an annual festival, Lockport Old Canal Days, the third weekend of every June. Both the Gaylord Donnelley and Dellwood Park trails are open for cross-country skiing. A self-guided walking tour map of historic Lockport describes 32 points of interest. For more information call the Lockport Township Park District at 815-838-1183 or the Lockport Chamber of Commerce at 815-838-3357.

Centennial Trail

A new NHC trail, under development at the time of writing, will become a gateway for Chicagoland trail users to visit and enjoy the many attractions and points of interest along the I&M Canal. The Centennial Trail, when completed, will run for 20 miles from the Chicago Portage site at Lyons in Cook County to Lockport in Will County. The 10-foot-wide trail will also be a key link in the 500+ mile Grand Illinois Trail targeted for completion in the year 2000. (See Section 23.) Construction of the Centennial Trail is planned in Cook, DuPage, and Will Counties. Approximately three miles of the trail are already open in Will County from the Cook County line to the Isle a la Cache Museum east of Romeoville.

How to get there:

The planned northern trailhead for the Centennial Trail will be located at the Chicago Portage National Historic Site in Lyons. Take Harlem Avenue south of Ogden Avenue and Joliet Avenue to 47th Street in Lyons. The entrance will be to the west. The southern trailhead is at 2nd Street in Lockport where the planned Centennial Trail will connect with the existing Gaylord Donnelley Canal Trail described in Section 10.

Chicago Portage/Ottawa Trail Woods

If you want to see where Jolliet and Marquette discovered a connection between the Great Lakes and the Mississippi River, hike through the 300-acre Ottawa Trail Woods Preserve and Chicago Portage Woods in Lyons.

How to get there:

Take Harlem Avenue south of Joliet Road. The first entrance to the west is for Ottawa Trail Woods Preserve parking area. A bit farther south on Harlem is the Chicago Portage Woods parking area.

At Chicago Portage Woods is a National Historic Site with a monument honoring Marquette and Jolliet. You can take the short footpath to Portage Creek to the south and another out to the Des Plaines River to the west. See the history section for more about the Chicago Portage.

In Ottawa Trail Woods, you will find a footpath along the river leading to Laughton's Ford. Two hundred years ago, Indian trails radiated out from this focal point, one to Grosse Point, present-day Wilmette, and another southwest to Ottawa. An interpretive facility is planned at Laughton's Ford near the river. This center will include a museum, a library, a replica of the old Laughton's Trading Post, and an archaeological facility.

From the portage site, the Centennial Trail will run on the north side of the Des Plaines River heading south to Willow Springs Road. After a bridge crossing over the river, the trail continues southwest between the river and the Chicago Sanitary & Ship Canal parallel to the existing Cook County I&M Canal Bicycle Trail described in Section 20. At the time of writing, a trail bridge was recently installed over the Chicago Sanitary & Ship Canal as part of the construction of a new Route 83 auto bridge. This new trail bridge will connect the Centennial Trail to Cook County's I&M Canal Bicycle Trail. Southeast of here lie the beautiful 14,000-acre Palos Preserves filled with hiking and biking trails. See Section 19.

West of Palos, the Centennial Trail will enter DuPage County near the Waterfall Glen Forest Preserve, which contains an excellent 9.5-mile loop trail around Argonne National Laboratory (see Section 17). After a 2.5-mile stretch through DuPage County, the trail briefly re-enters the southwest corner of Cook County north of Lemont. The path will proceed southwest through Lemont and connect to Lemont's canal trail. (See Section 16.)

In Will County, a 3-mile section of the Centennial Trail is open from the Cook/Will County line to 135th Street in Romeoville near the Isle a la Cache Museum. In part, it crosses over an old swing bridge salvaged from the Chicago Sanitary and Ship Canal. The Forest Preserve District of Will County (FPDWC) plans to upgrade the trail surface with limestone screenings.

Isle a la Cache Museum

An 80-acre island in the Des Plaines River is home to an excellent museum that celebrates the French/Native American fur trade that prospered in the mid-18th century.

How to get there:

Take Route 53 to Romeo Road in Romeoville. Head east for .5 mile. The museum entrance is to the south. From the east, take 135th Street west of Archer Avenue/Route 171 after the road project mentioned below is completed.

At the time of writing, a major road project was underway here. Three new bridges were under construction on Romeo Road as well as the creation of a new four-lane highway to connect with 135th Street to the east. Two bridges cross over the Des Plaines River on each side of the island. A third bridge crosses over the Sanitary and Ship Canal. Hopefully, by the time you read this, the bridge and road construction will be complete.

Native Americans camped on the island when they traveled the Des Plaines River for trade or hunting. The FPDWC has created an interpretive site that commemorates those Native Americans as well as the early French traders who sought the valuable beaver pelts so popular for top hats for European gentlemen of that era. In the well laid out museum, you can see replicas of the canoes they used, the

Island Rendezvous at Isle a la Cache.

trinkets they traded, a beaver lodge, and a display of the extensive trade routes that developed in the 18th century. You will also find two short hiking trails near the museum. Hours are 10 a.m. to 4 p.m. Tuesday–Saturday, Noon to 4 p.m. on Sunday, closed Monday. Call 815-886-1467 for more information.

The plan is to extend the Centennial Trail 2.8 miles from Isle a la Cache south to 2nd Street in Lockport where it will connect with the existing 2.3-mile Gaylord Donnelley Canal Trail through downtown Lockport. With the completion of the Centennial Trail, the Heritage Trail, and the I&M Canal State Trail extension, hikers and bicyclists will have access to an 88-mile backbone corridor of off-road trails and pathways filled with natural greenways, recreational opportunities, and history. Plus, the other nearby trail systems mentioned above offer many additional miles of pathways to explore.

Canoeists will enjoy the 20-mile Chicago Portage Canoe Trail from Stony Ford in Lyons to Isle a la Cache Museum in Will County. Call the Forest Preserve District of Cook County at 708-366-9420 for more information and a canoe trail map.

An Island Rendezvous is held in June each year at Isle a la Cache sponsored by the FPDWC. Where else can you enjoy activities ranging from a tomahawk-throwing contest to canoe races to storytelling and puppet shows. Re-enactors in period clothing help visitors understand what life was like in the 1750s. Admission is free. Call 815-727-8700 for more information.

Southwestern Will County Forest Preserve Trails

Southwestern Will County is filled with a vast amount of open land and water dedicated as preserves and greenways. Here you will find the recently established 19,500-acre Midewin National Tallgrass Prairie, the 5,012-acre Des Plaines Conservation Area, the Kankakee, DuPage, and Des Plaines Rivers, the I&M Canal, and many creeks and streams, as well as three Will County forest preserves. (See Will County map on page 18.) As new homes and businesses are being developed throughout Will County, these natural areas will become priceless. And because many of them are dedicated Illinois Nature Preserves, they are protected forever from disturbance. A word needs to be said here about the Illinois Nature Preserves Commission. This group, formed in 1963, was created to protect the distinctive ecosystems existing in Illinois that provide resting, feeding, and breeding places to many threatened and endangered species. Most of the Illinois' 236+ dedicated nature preserves are open to the public. You will find quite a few in the Will County forest pre- serves. Explore these

Forest Preserve District of Will County

McKinley Woods trail.

areas to enjoy some of our state's rare wildlife, but please remember to be kind to these fragile environments.

McKinley Woods

One of the most scenic and one of my favorite preserves in Will County is at a large bend in the Des Plaines River south of Channahon. A short distance north of 473-acre McKinley Woods, in Channahon, the DuPage River empties into the Des Plaines and thus increases its size and strength. As you enter McKinley Woods, the road leads through an upland forest and then down a steep hill into the river valley.

On my first visit a large group of Girl Scouts was just finishing a camp-out. The parking area at Boatsman Landing was a beehive of activity. McKinley Woods is a popular spot for trail users for two reasons. First, it is an excellent location to access the I&M Canal State Trail that runs through the preserve. (See Section 1.) Secondly, there are 2.5 miles of packed earth hiking trails overlooking ravines, the canal, and the river.

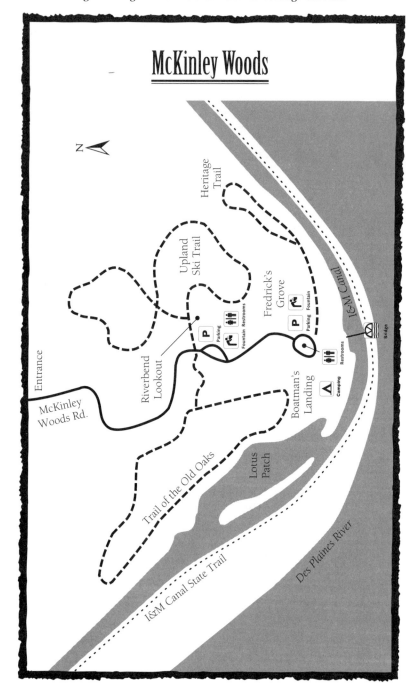

McKinley Woods

How to get there:

The best way is by hiking or biking the I&M Canal State Trail. By motorized vehicle, take I-55 to Route 6 northeast of Channahon. Exit on Route 6 heading west. McKinley Woods Road is 3.5 miles west of I-55. Head south on McKinley Woods Road for 2 miles through a new housing development to the preserve entrance.

From the entrance, head downhill to the Boatsman Landing parking area. This is a good place to park for either the McKinley Woods trails or the nearby I&M Canal State Trail. Access to the state trail is a short distance to the south across the canal. Shelters, a water pump, and restrooms are nearby. East of Boatsman Landing is Frederick's Grove and access to the .5 mile Heritage Trail. The packed earth path heads through an oak/maple woodland northeast along the I&M Canal. You will pass by an old limestone shelter built by the Civilian Conservation Corps during the Depression. Watch for roots and stones on the trail. As I walked farther into the forest, the only sound I heard came from a squirrel scampering through the fallen oak leaves. Soon I came to an intersection, which is the beginning of a loop. The path right continued along the canal. As the trail turned north, it also started a fairly steep climb. The return portion ran even farther up the hill (see map).

Back at Boatsman Landing, access to the 1.2-mile Trail of the Old Oaks is west of the parking lot beyond a large mowed turf area. This trail has a steep climb with some scenic views of the canal, river, and later deep ravines. A spur to the left leads east to the River Bend Lookout parking area. The Trail of the Old Oaks continues to the right back down the valley to Boatsman Landing. East of the Riverbend Lookout parking area is the Upland Ski Trail consisting of two loops totaling .8 mile.

Your motor vehicle may be left overnight if you are planning on camping or lodging along the I&M Canal State Trail. You need to notify the Forest Preserve District of Will County at 815-727-8700. Two miles of trails are open for cross-country skiing in the winter.

Forsythe Woods

Jordan and Forked Creeks merge in the northwestern section of this

114-acre preserve and, from there, flow west 1.5 miles to join the Kankakee River. The community of Wilmington is north of the preserve.

How to get there:

Take Route 53 to Route 102 near the Kankakee River in Wilmington. Take Route 102 southeast for .7 mile to Kahler Road. Head east (left) for .9 mile to the preserve entrance on your left.

There are 2 miles of hiking trails through woodland and grasslands at this 114-acre preserve. A site map on the information signboard next to the parking area shows the overlapping loop trails. Head north past the shelter through the mowed turf area to access the woodland trails. Forsythe Woods is open for cross-country skiing. You will find water, a shelter, picnic tables, restrooms, and horseshoe pits near the parking area.

Braidwood Dunes & Savanna Nature Preserve

A black oak savanna, a dunesland, and a sand prairie await you at this 288-acre state-dedicated Illinois Nature Preserve, west of the Kankakee River and east of the community of Braidwood.

Here you will find one of the largest and most diverse examples of dry-mesic sand savannas in Illinois. The savanna features some unusual species including the woodbine, an understory climbing vine, and the huckleberry. At the dune ridges, you may discover the prickly pear cactus, which features yellow blooms atop its scratchy green cactus-like foliage in summer. The dunes and savanna vegetation provides home to a wide array of mammals, reptiles, amphibians, and birds. One interesting species is the tiger salamander. They breed in late winter when ponds begin to thaw. The female attaches her egg masses to underwater debris in temporary pools, then leaves. The larvae feed and grow through spring and early summer. Search for them at dusk in summer when the young come out to feed. Salamanders make a nice meal for many animals such as snakes, turtles, herons, and fish. They, in turn, feed on insects, earthworms, small mice, and even other amphibians. They avoid predators by leading secret lifestyles and emerging only under the cover of darkness.

How to get there:

Take Route 113 east of Route 53 and I-55 for .5 mile east of Braidwood. A gravel road leads to the parking area south of Route 113. The trailhead is south of the parking area.

A 1-mile packed earth and sand loop trail is bisected by a cutback trail thereby forming a .5-mile loop. See the map on the information signpost. On an August hike, I walked amid a sea of wildflowers as monarch butterflies and bumblebees dined on the flowers' nectar. Periodic burns rejuvenate the prairie forbs and grasses. Unusual species such as the prickly pear cactus, yellow-eyed grass, and the state threatened tubercle orchid grow here. The prairie landscape quickly changed to mostly dunesland. As I headed east, the trail was bordered to the south by a beautiful oak savanna. Young saplings grew everywhere. A small dried creekbed on the south side of the preserve paralleled the trail for a short distance. Heading back north toward the parking area, the pathway led through the edge of a silver maple woodland.

I must have walked over at least 10 to 15 mole tunnels on the short 1-mile hike. Berry bushes with a mixture of deep purple, bright red, and a few unripened green berries lined the trail.

There is little shade for most of the hike. Also there are no facilities at Braidwood except for the parking lot and a port-a-john in the summer. The preserve is a bit isolated. But it's certainly worth visiting.

Northwestern Will County Forest Preserve Trails

The Des Plaines and the DuPage Rivers served as major transportation routes for Native Americans and French fur traders. The two rivers are somewhat parallel as they meander south through northwestern Will County. Six forest preserves situated along or near the rivers offer trails and other activities for your enjoyment.

Keepataw Preserve

Starting with the farthest north and heading south, the 216-acre Keepataw Preserve, south of Bolingbrook and I-55, overlooks the Des Plaines River Valley.

How to get there:

Take Route 53 north of Romeoville and south of I-55. Take Joliet Road north to Bluff Road. Turn right (east). The preserve entrance is on the south side of Bluff Road, 1 mile east of Joliet Road.

A short .3-mile mowed turf trail loops through a new growth woodland on a high bluff overlooking the Des Plaines. You will find a scenic overlook of the river valley half way around the loop. There is a bench for you to sit and enjoy the view. No facilities are at this site.

Veterans Woods

Southwest of Keepataw is a 77-acre preserve along busy Joliet Road.

How to get there:

Take Joliet Road south of I-55 and north of Romeoville. The preserve is one mile south of I-55. There are two preserve entrances, Acorn Grove and Trader's Corners. I parked at Acorn Grove, the entrance farther south.

Beautiful tall oaks are scattered throughout the grassy area near the shelter. Access to a .3-mile packed earth trail is to the left across a bridge. The trail runs downhill into a large ravine. The creek bed at the bottom was dry during my summer visits.

Lake Renwick Heron Rookery Nature Preserve

Bring your binoculars when you visit this Illinois Nature Preserve. What was once a quarry for gravel mining operations, now is a home for egrets and herons. From spring until fall, great blue heron, black-crowned night-herons, cattle egrets, great egrets, and double-crested cormorants nest on two small islands in the middle of 200-acre Lake Renwick. During the breeding season, there are over 500 nests crammed together for safety, the great blue herons occupying the top floor. You can hear and observe the interesting antics of these species, the adults clicking their bills together to establish pair bonds, the adults gathering sticks in which to build their nests, the young cackling as they beg to be fed, their parents flying off, sometimes as far as 40 miles away to find a meal.

Here's how to recognize these species. The great blue heron is the largest, reaching 4-feet tall. It has a white head, crest, and gray body, and flies with a folded neck. The great egret has long, black legs and a yellow bill and is about 3-feet tall. In the 1900s, this species was nearly hunted to extinction for its beautiful, white feathers used in women's hats. In fact, the National Audubon Society was formed to save the great egret. The cattle egret is less than 2-feet tall, and dons orange on its white breast and head during breeding season. This species nests close to the ground, while the great blue heron chooses the top bunk and the great egret selects the middle.

Also look for black-crowned night-herons. This species is about 2-feet tall and has a black crown with white underparts. It feeds at night. Finally, look for the double-crested cormorant, which dives under water to catch fish, then sits in a tree spreading its wings so the feathers can dry. This species was once endangered in Illinois, but is now much more common.

How to get there:

From Route 59 in Plainfield, take Route 30 (Plainfield Road) southeast to Renwick Road. Turn left (east). The preserve entrance is .5 mile east of Route 30 on the north side of the road.

From the parking area, a short .2-mile crushed gravel hiking trail leads through a small woodland to the viewing area. The birds can be sensitive to visitor actions. Signs caution no dogs, loud noises, running or venturing off the path. While the trail here is short, a visit is very worthwhile. This breeding ground is unique in northern Illinois.

Viewing times are limited from May to August on Saturday from 8 a.m. to noon and on Wednesday at 10 a.m. The preserve is open only during these hours. A forest preserve district naturalist gives scheduled tours and presentations. Spotting scopes are provided for use during the viewing. Be sure to register at the visitor center. Lake Renwick is co-owned by the Illinois Department of Natural Resources and the Forest Preserve District of Will County. Call 815-727-8700 for more information.

Lockport Prairie Nature Preserve

Along the west bank of the Des Plaines River in Lockport, a restored prairie flourishes.

How to get there:

Take Route 53 south of Route 7/9th Street to Division Street in the outskirts of Lockport. Head east to the trailhead near an information signpost along the road.

Division Street dead ends east of the prairie at a blockade of an abandoned bridge across the Des Plaines. You can park your car along the road by the trailhead or farther west at a pullout along the road.

Lockport Prairie, a 254-acre state nature preserve, is composed of a variety of environments, dry prairie, marsh, fen, and sedge meadow. The trail, a short .4-mile linear route to the south, is a narrow, mowed turf hiking path. There are no facilities at this site.

One of the most unique features of the Lockport Prairie is that it harbors the federally endangered leafy prairie-clover. Before scientists discovered the clover here, it had not been recorded in Illinois for more than 70 years. Leafy prairie-clover has erect, 1-foot stems. Small purple flowers bloom in dense spikes at the end of the stems beginning in late July. In fall, the dead stems remain erect and disperse ripened seeds. The species grows in prairie remnants that occur on thin-soil areas overlying dolomite. The type of community present at Lockport Prairie has almost completely disappeared from the Midwest. We are fortunate to still have it, and obligated to protect it.

Rock Run Preserve-Black Road Access

Big bluestem and goldenrod, can be found in the prairie here. Water fowl visit the ponds and wetland at this former quarry west of Joliet.

How to get there:

From I-55, take the Jefferson Street exit east to Route 7. Head north on Route 7 to Black Road. Turn left (west) on Black. The preserve entrance is labeled Black Road Access.

A 1.2-mile asphalt trail with interpretive signposts loops around the wetland. Two short .4-mile crushed limestone side trails run through a sedge meadow and a prairie.

A white egret was searching for food on the pond as I passed by. Rock Run Creek flows through the preserve on its way south where it empties into the I&M Canal. This is one of the few streams that does so.

The trails at Black Road Access will be extended in late 1998–1999 as part of the Rock Run Greenway development. A .7-mile asphalt segment leading to a short on-road section followed by another asphalt segment (.8 mile) will offer trail users more natural areas to explore.

Lower Rock Run-I&M Canal Access

Southwest of Joliet is a recently opened Will County forest preserve that provides access to the new section of the I&M Canal State Trail from I-55 to Brandon Road Lock & Dam. Hopefully the trail addition will be completed by the time you read this.

How to get there:

Take I-55 north of I-80 to the Jefferson Street exit. Head east to Houbolt Road. Turn right (south) on Houbolt. Proceed south for 3.1 miles passing under I-80. Houbolt becomes Bush Road south of I-80. The preserve entrance is to your right. From the south, you can take Route 6 to Bush Road. The entrance is .3 mile north of Route 6.

A .2-mile crushed limestone path heads southwest from the large parking area to a boardwalk and wooden deck. This observation area overlooking Rock Run is a great place to see beavers at work as well as other wildlife. Prairie and woodland restoration are underway. An asphalt pathway heads north of the parking area to the I&M Canal State Trail and the I&M Canal. (See Section 1.) A shelter, water pump, and latrine are available.

Hammel Woods

The DuPage River meanders through the eastern side of this 297-acre preserve. Here you will find three miles of trails that run on high bluffs along the river and through woodland.

How to get there:

Take Route 59 north of Route 52/Jefferson Street. There are two entrances. One is on Route 59, .6 mile north of Route 52. The other is on Black Road .2 mile east of Route 59 at the Crumby Recreation Area entrance.

If you enter from Black Road, use the first parking area near the entrance. Beyond the restrooms you will find a trail sign at a three-way intersection that directs trail users to the southern section of the preserve, to the DuPage River, and to the Crumby Recreation Area. Trail markers help guide you.

If you enter the preserve from Route 59, an auto road winds south

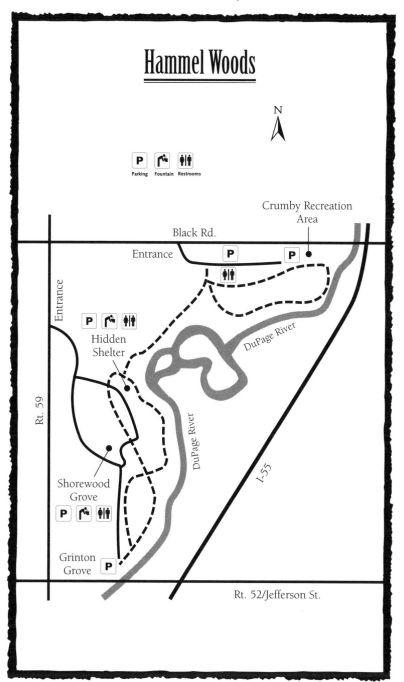

Hammel Woods

N

P Parking Fountain Restrooms

Crumby Recreation Area

Black Rd.

Entrance P   P

Entrance

Hidden Shelter

DuPage River

Shorewood Grove

Rt. 59

DuPage River

I-55

Grinton Grove P

Rt. 52/Jefferson St.

Forest Preserve District of Will County

Dam at Hammel Woods.

through Hammel Woods with parking areas near the trails at three sites: Hidden Shelter, Shorewood Grove, and Grinton Grove. As I drove south to Grinton Grove on a sunny fall day, the vibrant gold and yellow hues of the tall maple trees caught my eye.

From the Grinton Grove parking area, a short walk east over an old stone bridge will take you to a nice view of a dam on the DuPage River. Nearby, a .5-mile packed earth loop trail heads north through an oak/maple woodland to Shorewood Grove where it connects to a 1-mile loop trail that continues north to Hidden Shelter. The eastern side of these loop trails offers a climb first up and then along a bluff high above the river. Great view!

Water, picnic tables, shelters, and restrooms are available near the parking areas. Family camping is available near the DuPage River. Call 815-727-8700 for more information.

Rock Run and Hammel Woods are open for cross-country skiing.

Northcentral Will County Hiking & Biking Trails

East of Joliet and Lockport you will find three preserves with beautiful woodlands and meadows to explore.

Hickory Creek Preserve

The Forest Preserve District of Will County's largest site is 1,800-acre Hickory Creek Preserve south of Mokena and north of Frankfort. The stream that bears its name runs through the preserve on its way west to the Des Plaines River. The preserve is divided into two sections by Wolf Road. The eastern section includes a 1.8-mile asphalt hiking and biking trail as well as two short packed earth or mowed turf hiking-only trails that loop off the main trail (see map). The hiking trails total .9 mile.

How to get there:

A good place to park to reach the trails on the east side of Hickory Creek is at the La Porte Road Access entrance in Mokena. Take Wolf Road 1.8 miles north of Route 30 to La Porte Road. Turn right. The preserve entrance is .9 mile east of Wolf Road. Drive past the Hickory Hollow and Shagbark Grove shelters to the farthest south parking area.

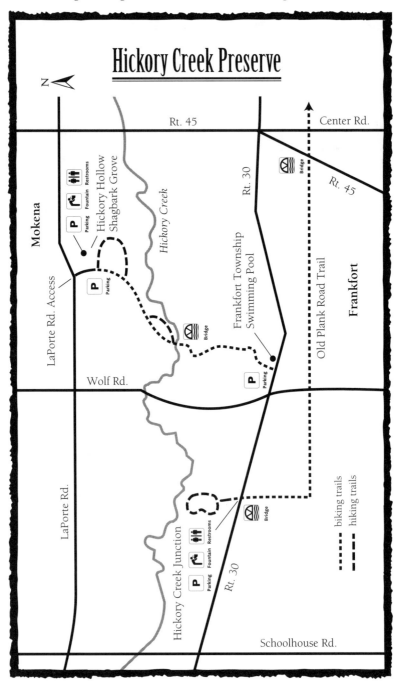

Bridge over Hickory Creek.

The 1.8-mile multi-use trail heads south from the La Porte Road parking area. The pathway leads downhill through an open meadow. A long bridge crosses over Hickory Creek as you enter a forest. Tall oak trees line the path. The trail is relatively hilly and features a couple of good climbs along the way. The path ends at the Frankfort Township Swimming Pool at Route 30 where parking is also available. Restrooms and a water pump are available at Hickory Hollow Shelter north of the trailhead parking area. The asphalt trail is open for cross-country skiing.

West of Wolf Road, at Hickory Creek Junction, you will find the trailhead for the Old Plank Road Trail, as well as a 1-mile hiking trail.

How to get there:

Take Lincoln Highway (Route 30) west of Route 45 or east of Cedar Road. The Hickory Creek Junction entrance is to the north. A long pedestrian bridge over Route 30 is the beginning of a connector leading to the Old Plank Road Trail. (See Section 9 for more information.) North of the Old Plank Road trailhead parking area you will find a 1-mile mowed turf hiking trail that loops through a large open meadow. A water pump, restrooms, and more parking are available here.

Additional trails are planned at Hickory Creek Preserve during the next few years. Hickory Creek is home to the forest preserve district's Environmental Learning Center. Adult educational workshops are offered here year-round covering a wide variety of environmental subjects. Call 708-479-2255 for more information.

Messenger Woods Nature Preserve

Near Orland Park is a peaceful, secluded spot called Messenger Woods. Spring Creek runs through this 947-acre state-dedicated nature preserve noted for beautiful spring wildflowers and rare nesting bird species. Messenger Woods is on the Illinois Natural Area Inventory list because of its high-quality dry-mesic and mesic upland forest. Other plant communities present within the preserve include shrub swamp, wet prairie, and cultural communities. At least 146 native plant species have been recorded here, including the state-endangered rock elm, though this species may already be gone from the site. When you walk through the preserve in spring and early summer, listen for the spiraling, flute-like call of the state-threatened veery, a lovely chocolate brown thrush that has nested here. You might also here the strident "kleeyur" call of the state-endangered red-shouldered hawk, which has also nested nearby.

How to get there:

Messenger Woods is east of Lockport and west of Will Cook Road. Take Cedar Road north of Route 6 or south of Route 7 to Bruce Road. Head east on Bruce staying left at the Y. The preserve entrance is to the north. Take the auto road to either of the two parking areas.

In spring, wildflowers fill the forest floor at this nature sanctuary. At the first shelter area, Oak Knoll, you can access a 1.3-mile loop trail. The trailhead is southeast of the parking area. Look for the trail marker. A short connector leads to the loop trail (see map). I took the packed earth pathway south through a mature oak and maple forest. This is a quiet, serene spot with little traffic sounds. The relatively flat

Messenger Woods Nature Preserve

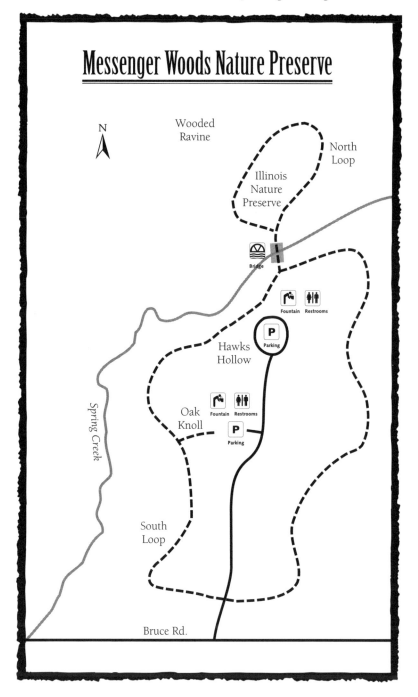

trail crosses the auto road and turns north. Here the forest is mostly new growth. At the Hawthorn Shelter area, you will come to a clearing and the trailhead for a .5-mile nature trail.

The northern section of the preserve is a designated Illinois Nature Preserve and is not open for pets. To hike the nature trail mentioned above, cross the stone bridge over Spring Creek and head north along a ridge overlooking a ravine. Here the terrain is a bit more hilly. In spring, the forest floor is filled with white trillium, bloodroot, blue-eyed Mary, and Virginia bluebells. On an early September hike, we saw a giant puffball mushroom the size of a bowling ball.

You will find water, picnic tables, shelters, and restrooms at both the Hawthorn and Oak Knoll areas.

Homer Trails at Spring Creek Preserve

The Forest Preserve District of Will County has established an equestrian trail at Spring Creek Preserve east of Lockport. The 3.2-mile pathway is also open to hikers.

How to get there:

Take Bell Road .4 mile south of Route 7/159th Street. Bell Road-South is a short distance east of Bell Road-North on Route 7.

The trail consists of three loops with connector segments that tie the loops together. The 10-foot-wide pathway runs through open meadow. Part of the trail runs along a mature oak forest and overlooks Spring Creek.The trail surface is a mixture of crushed limestone, mowed turf, packed earth, and some loose gravel. The path is bumpy in spots so wear sturdy shoes or hiking boots. In late September, grasshoppers bounded across the path as monarchs feasted on the flowers' nectar. These and other insects are a vital part of the ecosystem, providing food for birds and mammals, as well as pollinating plants.

Hickory Creek Preserve, Messenger Woods, and Homer Trails at Spring Creek Preserve are all open for cross-country skiing when the snows come.

Eastern Will County Forest Preserve Hiking Trails

Amid the farmland of Will County east of I-57, south of Lincoln Highway (Route 30), and close to the Indiana border you will find peaceful hiking trails at four preserves.

Goodenow Grove Forest Preserve

Will County's eastern-most preserve is south of Crete and less than 5 miles from Indiana. Several loop hiking trails totaling 3.5 miles surround the Plum Creek Nature Center.

How to get there:

Take Goodenow Road 1.2 miles east of the intersection of Routes 1 and 394. Turn left (north) on Dutton Road. The preserve entrance is to the left. Follow the auto road to the Plum Creek Nature Center.

At the nature center, named for the creek that flows through the preserve, you will find environmental exhibits and displays. Children will enjoy the Discovery Den, a hands-on place where they can learn more about nature.

A 1-mile gravel loop trail starts west of the nature center and heads north through Thorn

Apple Meadow, then loops back to the nature center. A 1-mile packed earth hiking trail heads east off of the gravel trail through a woodland. Three shorter loop trails of .3 to .5 mile are to the north, west, and south of the center. At the time of writing, a .3-mile wheelchair accessible, interpretive trail, the Trail of Thoughts, was under construction starting at the Nodding Oaks picnic area near the nature center. A big sledding hill sits in the middle of the preserve. Climb it for a nice panoramic view of the surrounding countryside.

A public phone, restrooms, and water fountain are available at the nature center. Here you can pick up a trail map as well as many other brochures. Both family and group camping sites are available at Goodenow Grove. A cross-country ski trail is open in winter. Several miles of additional trails are planned here. Call 708-946-2216 for more information.

Monee Reservoir

Built on what was once mostly farmland along Rock Creek, the reservoir helps control flooding and provides a water recreation area for fishing and boating. The adjoining wetlands attract waterfowl and other animals. On my first visit, a great blue heron took to flight from a wetland as I walked by.

How to get there:

Take Governors Highway (Route 50) 2 miles south of Monee or north of Peotone to Pauling Road. Head west on Pauling .7 mile to Ridgeland Avenue. Turn left on Ridgeland and proceed south .3 mile to the entrance on the left. Park in the lot near the concession/information center.

East of the parking area near the boat dock, you will find access to 2 miles of mowed turf hiking trail through a wetland north of the lake. As I walked on the path through the wetland restoration area, a red-winged blackbird flew close above me for some distance screeching incessantly, leaving me with a definite feeling that my presence was not welcome. It was no doubt a parent protecting a nearby nest. North of the wetland area is a .5-mile loop trail through a meadow. Also a short asphalt walking path runs along the lake by the boat dock.

At the concession/information center, row boats and pedal boats are available for rental as are horseshoes. The center is open 6 a.m. to 7 p.m. from April through October and 8 a.m. to 4 p.m. November through March. The concession stand is closed on Mondays. Water, a public telephone, a bike rack, and restrooms are available. Shelters and picnic tables are nearby at Bluegill Hill. Call 708-534-8499 for more information.

While Monee Reservoir and Raccoon Grove Nature Preserve are adjoining, these trails do not connect. The preserves are separated by the Illinois Central Gulf railroad tracks and Route 50.

Raccoon Grove Nature Preserve

East of Monee Reservoir is a 210-acre woodland with a tranquil hiking trail.

How to get there:

Take Governors Highway (Route 50) south of Monee or north of Peotone to Pauling Road. The entrance is on Pauling at the Route 50

Raccoon Grove Nature Preserve.

intersection.

Raccoon Grove features upland and floodplain forests dominated by white, bur and black oak and shagbark hickory in the drier sections as well as red and white oak and sugar maple in the wetter areas. As you hike the area, notice how the tree types change when you move from drier to wetter areas.

Raccoon Grove has been designated an Illinois Nature Preserve to protect the flora and fauna that reside here. A .5-mile packed earth trail crosses over Rock Creek on a small wooden bridge and loops through a mature maple forest. Here the creek is a small stream usually dry in the summer. Farther south, in Kankakee River State Park, you can see the creek again as a grown up stream lined with tall limestone cliffs. (See Section 6.)

Thorn Creek Woods Nature Preserve

In Park Forest near the Cook County line is an 850-acre Illinois Nature Preserve. Woodlands, prairie, and wetlands flourish at Thorn Creek. This is an excellent spot for a quiet walk on the 2.5 miles of packed earth hiking trails that meander through the preserve.

You can hike through upland ravine areas where white oaks grow and ravine bottomlands where sugar maple, black maple, and basswood thrive. Also notice the understory of interesting shrubs such as the witch hazel, hawthorns, viburnums, and blackhaw. This is truly a feast for the eyes. The best time to learn your trees and shrubs is in the fall when their nuts and fruits as well as next year's buds are developed. You can also examine acorns to identify oak trees. For example, the Hill's oak has a long, elliptical acorn with a deep, scaly cap, while the black oak's acorn has a conical cap with a rusty fringe.

Spring wildflowers abound here, too, including the orange and yellow-hued columbine, which attracts migrating hummingbirds to its tube-like flowers. Also breeding in the wet areas are blue-spotted salamanders.

How to get there:

From the east take Exchange Road west of Route 1 and Western Avenue to Old Monee Road. Head north for .9 mile. The entrance is

Thorn Creek Nature Preserve

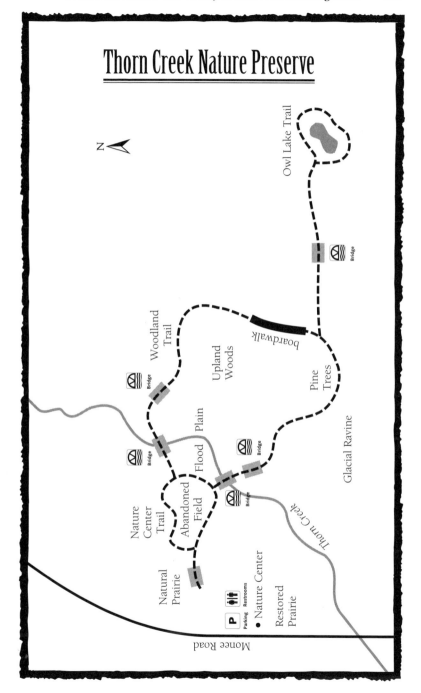

on the right. From the west, take Governors Highway to Stuenkel Road. Head east to Old Monee Road. Turn left (north) on Old Monee.

Seasonal trail guides are available at the information signpost near the trailhead next to the nature center. A .5-mile trail loops around a field where a prairie is being restored. To the east this short trail connects with the 1.3-mile Woodland Trail through the floodplain of Thorn Creek. Tall sugar maple, elm, black walnut, and red oak surround the path. Here the trail runs along a bluff high above a large ravine. On the southern section of the loop, a stand of tall white pines surrounds the trail. A rust-colored carpet of pine needles offers a soft hiking surface and provides a vivid contrast to the surrounding greenery.

East of the pine grove is a trail intersection with a spur heading farther east to a small pond filled with cattails. This part of the trail can be somewhat overgrown in summer. After looping around Owl Lake, return to the trail intersection. Assuming you took the southern route out, take the path to the right which leads to a long boardwalk. The forest is filled with wildflowers in the spring. Spring beauty, dutchman's breeches, and Virginia bluebells grow here. On the north side of the Woodland Trail, I heard a loud constant buzzing noise coming from a nearby nest. The naturalist told me that paper wasps and bald-faced hornets make their home in the woods here.

A bike rack, water fountain, and latrine are near the trailhead and parking lot. No dogs, cross-country skiing, or bikes are allowed on the trails. The nature center occupies an old church. Here you will find interesting nature displays, books, and a bird-feeding station. Programs are offered year-round. The nature center is open from noon to 4 p.m., Thursday through Sunday. Call 708-747-6320 for more information.

Lemont/Romeoville Area Trails

Several things draw your attention as you drive
down into the Des Plaines River Valley on
Lemont Road entering the historic community of
Lemont. First there are all the beautiful spires of
churches rising above the trees. Secondly, there is
the large number of gritty storage tanks along the
waterways. Thirdly, there is the long bridge into
downtown Lemont, first crossing the Des Plaines
River, then the Chicago Sanitary and Ship Canal,
and lastly the relatively narrow I&M Canal. The
waterways clearly have played a key role in the
development of this community. Immigrants
from Ireland, Sweden, and Germany moved here
in the 1830s and 1840s to work on the I&M
Canal. People of other nationalities came later.

Lemont's I&M Canal Walk

A 3.4-mile linear multi-use path runs along
the I&M Canal in downtown Lemont south of
the Chicago Sanitary and Ship Canal.

How to get there:

Take Lemont Road south of I-55 or State Street
north of Route 171 (Archer Avenue) into downtown Lemont. Head east on Illinois Street to
Stephen Street. Turn left (north). Trail access is

three blocks north after crossing the I&M Canal. Trail parking is available along the canal near the Water Reclamation Plant.

The village built a crushed limestone path along the I&M Canal as well as General Fry's Landing, a small park, named in honor of Jacob Fry, an early canal commissioner. Here you will find benches, street lights, and a small Friendship Garden. The trail runs northeast for 1.3 miles. Watch for mileage markers. On my first visit, yellow daisies grew along the pathway near the dolomite-lined canal banks. The stone foundations from a long-gone bridge still stand. You will need to backtrack to Fry's Landing south of Stephen Street. Watch out for glass on the trail. I followed the trail southwest along the canal for 2.1 miles past a huge steel mill to the north. There are currently no water fountains or restrooms along the trail. However, there are several restaurants nearby.

Lemont's Canal Walk will parallel but not be a part of the Centennial Trail (Section 11) which was under development at the time of writing. A walking tour on the sidewalks of downtown Lemont points out restored landmarks and other items of interest. Call 630-257-1550 for more information.

Black Partridge Forest Preserve

Black Partridge, a Cook County forest preserve, north of the Des Plaines River near Lemont, is a good place to see spring wildflowers and forest-dwelling birds such as the red-headed woodpecker.

How to get there:

Take Lemont Road 1.9 miles south of I-55 or north of the State Street bridge in Lemont. Head west on Bluff Road 1.2 miles to a parking lot to the north at this 80-acre Illinois Nature Preserve. There are no marked trails here. A .5-mile packed earth footpath starting north of the parking area loops through the woods on a ridge along ravines and a small creek. In the spring, Virginia bluebells and white trillium carpet the forest floor. Listen for the plaintive call "pee-a-wee" of the eastern wood-pewee, a flycatcher that nests here. Or watch for a flash of red-white-and-black. This could be the red-headed wood-pecker, whose numbers are declining in this area. This particular species of woodpecker was once quite common in northern Illinois' oak savannas. Another rare species observed in this state nature preserve is the mottled sculpin, a small fish that dwells on the bottom of clean streams. The presence of this species indicates the high quality of the stream.

A short distance to the west across an old stone bridge, you will find a water fountain, restrooms, a shelter, and picnic tables.

O'Hara Woods Nature Preserve

Farther west in Romeoville is another popular spot for spring wildflowers. Forty-acre O'Hara Woods is owned by the Romeoville Recreation Department.

How to get there:

Take Route 53 to Romeoville. Head west on Romeo Road (135th Street) for approximately 1.5 miles. The preserve is located behind the Romeoville Recreation Department building at 900 W. Romeo Road. Park behind the building along the tennis courts.

The trailhead is the gravel road to the north. Three miles of unmarked packed earth trail loop through a maple and oak woodland. When my friend, Hank, and I visited in early August, quite a few mature trees had been uprooted after a severe storm. In the spring, you will see Virginia bluebells, skunk cabbage, and other wildflowers. The skunk cabbage is one of the earliest plants to emerge in spring in the Chicago region. In late March, several basal leaves begin to grow. The flowers bloom from early March to early May. The skunk-like odor of this plant attracts certain insects that feed upon the plant. Call 815-886-6222 for more information about O'Hara Woods.

Waterfall Glen Forest Preserve

A nearly pristine environment, Waterfall Glen encircles the Argonne National Laboratory in the southeastern part of DuPage County. I-55 runs along the northern border and Route 83 near the eastern side. South of the forest preserve on Route 83, you will encounter the conflux of the Santa Fe Railroad tracks, the Des Plaines River, the Chicago Sanitary and Ship Canal, the remnants of the historic I&M Canal, and two huge auto junk yards. With all this nearby civilization, it's hard to imagine much of an outdoors experience. But once on the 9.5-mile multi-use trail, the outside world is completely forgotten. This is one of Dupage County's most ecologically and scenically diverse areas. You'll find hilly ravines, rock outcroppings, a waterfall, and bluffs overlooking the Des Plaines River Valley.

Living in this 2,470-acre ring of wilderness are 75 percent of all plant species found in DuPage County. Ten endangered plants and 71 plants of special concern grow here. Scientists discovered the federally endangered Hines emerald dragon-

Forest Preserve District of DuPage County

Waterfall Glen Forest Preserve.

fly on the preserve.

There is so much to observe. On a hot humid spring evening, for instance, you might hear the call of the gray tree frog, a tiny woodland amphibian that breeds in marsh areas, then retreats to extensive woodland habitat for the summer's remainder.

Waterfall Glen, the only NHC site in DuPage County, is truly one of my favorites!

How to get there:

Take the Argonne National Laboratory/Cass Avenue exit (#273A) off I-55 heading south on Cass. Or take 91st Street 1.4 miles west of Route 83 to Cass Avenue heading north. Turn left at the Argonne National Laboratory Visitor's sign. Follow the sign to the Waterfall Glen Ski/Equestrian Trailhead parking area.

In addition to the main trail, there are many mowed turf trails, dirt paths, fire lanes, and service roads throughout the preserve offering miles of somewhat rugged pathways. These are often unmarked and largely unmapped. If you venture off on the side trails, bring a map and compass. Also, bicyclists are prohibited from trails less than 8-feet wide. Please stay on the trails to protect the environment of this beautiful preserve.

We describe the 9.5-mile multi-purpose trail, which consists mostly of crushed limestone surface. On the south side of the preserve, you will find a section of the main trail to be a mixture of packed earth, mowed turf, and narrow rock paths. Follow the trail markers at each intersection to help stay on the main trail. But, as mentioned above, a compass would be handy in case you miss a marker as I did. A crushed limestone surface will be installed on the rest of the main trial.

Following is a description heading west. The trail markers point out the main trail in both directions. You'll find water and restrooms at the trailhead. It's a good idea to partake since the next water fountain or restroom is ¾ of the way around the preserve at the Outdoor Education Camp area.

The Waterfall Glen trail, as well as being fairly long, is also very hilly. If you are cycling, a mountain or hybrid bike is preferable. There are some rough areas, washouts, and loose gravel on some parts of the main trail that are not yet crushed limestone. The trail leads mostly through beautiful woods of majestic oak and maple trees. Tall pines planted many years ago line the trail.

At 1.9 miles out, you'll come to Westgate Road and an employee entrance into Argonne. This research facility is funded by the U.S. Government for the physical, biomedical, and environmental sciences. Head right (west) on or along Westgate Road for .4 mile. The crushed limestone trail picks up again on the other side of the road. At 3.3 miles out is a large slough, a good place to watch wood ducks sitting on the half-submerged tree limbs.

At 3.7 miles out, you'll come to a rock road crossing (South Bluff Road). Head right (south) on the rock road for .1 mile. The trail resumes across the road next to a model airfield. On your left is the 80-acre Poverty Prairie named for the poverty oat grass that grows here along with mountain mint and pussytoes. To the right is the 200-acre Poverty Savannah with stately bur oaks rising above the tickle grass and yellow foxglove. Stay on the trail. The Forest Preserve

Waterfall Glen Forest Preserve

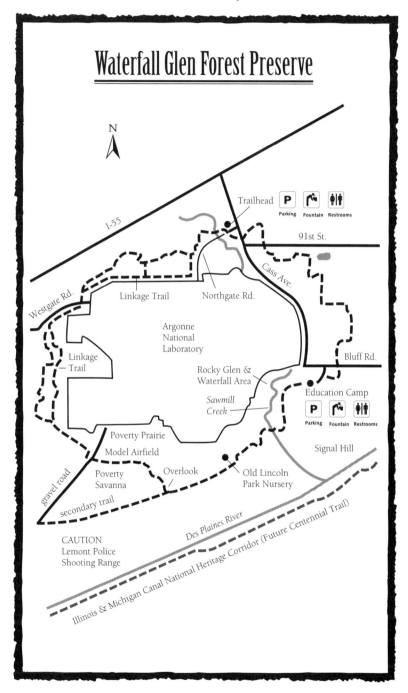

District brochure advises caution since the Lemont Police Department shooting range is south of the savanna. Near present-day Lemont, a French trader named DuPazhe, for whom the county is named, bartered with the Potowatami for furs.

At 4.7 miles out, the main trail climbs a hill to a "T" intersection. To the right along a service road is an information signpost and picnic table. You are now standing on top of a limestone bluff overlooking the Des Plaines River Valley to the south. There is a nice scenic view from this spot. In the late 19th and early 20th centuries, limestone quarries flourished in the river valley. You have most likely seen one of the buildings made from this limestone, the Chicago Water Tower on Michigan Avenue. In the early spring or winter, you can see the Des Plaines River below. In 1673, Louis Jolliet and Father Marquette canoed this area during their explorations. The service road leads out to South Bluff Road. To stay on the main trail follow the crushed limestone path to the left down the hill to the Santa Fe Railroad track.

You will pass by concrete walls and shells of buildings, remnants from the Lincoln Park Nursery. Plants were grown here and shipped, along with black topsoil, to Lincoln Park in Chicago. Cross the service road at 5.4 miles out. Follow the trail marker straight ahead leading to a trail bridge over Saw Mill Creek. Installed in 1997, this reroute of the main trail avoids a steep downhill loose gravel path to an older bridge nearby. From 1860 to 1880, the Ward brothers operated a sawmill near here. To the east is Signal Hill where Native Americans communicated via smoke signals.

As you head back north, you'll come to the Rocky Glen and waterfall area. A high bluff overlooks the creek below and offers a beautiful view at 6.3 miles out. But don't get too close to the edge. It is a long drop to the creekbed below. After you pass the information signpost, take the first side trail to your left down to the waterfall, which was built by the Civilian Conservation Corps in the 1930s. Note the trail is not open for bike riding. In dry periods, the water flow is only a trickle. But in the spring after a heavy rain, you can enjoy hearing the bubbling brook below the waterfall.

At 6.7 miles out, the main trail passes by the Outdoor Education Camp parking area off of Bluff Road. Here you'll find restrooms, drinking water, and a guard residence. The crushed limestone trail resumes here. Cross over Bluff Road at 6.9 miles and continue north. An information signpost at 8.3 miles out describes the "still hunting" technique used by Native Americans. Sit quietly and patiently, blend in with the environment, watch, and listen. You will probably observe many animals visiting the nearby wetland. The pine trees lining the far shore make this a picturesque spot.

As you head back west to complete the circle, you'll cross four more roads over the last mile of the trail at the forest preserve maintenance center, 91st Street, Cass Avenue, and Northgate Road.

In the winter, the multi-use trail is open for cross-country skiing. Since the main trail is quite hilly and long, beginners may want to start out with a flatter trail at one of the many other sites described in this guidebook. For the more accomplished skier, the trails here are a real delight. The Norsk Nordic Ski Patrol offers assistance to skiers on weekends when there is adequate snow cover.

Waterfall Glen Forest Preserve offers one of the most challenging and beautiful trails in the NHC. Call the Forest Preserve District of DuPage County at 630-790-4900 for more information.

Lake Katherine Nature Preserve

The community of Palos Heights has converted an area along the Calumet-Sag Channel from a dumping ground into a 158-acre nature preserve with a large lake, prairies, wetlands, a waterfall garden, 3.5 miles of hiking trails, and an Environmental Learning Center. This work earned the preserve a 1992 National Landscaping Award presented by former First Lady Barbara Bush.

How to get there:

South of the Calumet-Sag Channel, take Route 83 east of Route 45 to 75th Avenue or three blocks west of Harlem Avenue to 75th Avenue. The entrance is at the intersection of Route 83/College Drive and 75th Avenue/Lake Katherine Drive. On foot or bicycle, from the Tinley Creek Bicycle Trail at 131st Street, head north on the 2-mile asphalt bicycle path.

Preserve visitors will first encounter a picturesque waterfall and small rippling brook. Water from the nearby lake is pumped over to create a scenic and peaceful spot. Ducks swim in the pool at the bottom of the falls. Benches are nearby if you want to relax and enjoy. There are also small conifers as well as flower and butterfly gardens nearby. Butterflies rely on specific plants to lay their eggs and feed. On a warm, windless, sunny August day, you may see hundreds of these delicate creatures sipping nectar from annual and perennial flowers planted there to attract them. A walk on the 1-mile woodchip trail around 20-acre Lake Katherine leads to an overlook of the Calumet-Sag Channel, and recent plantings of spruce, pine, and deciduous trees to reforest the area. At the western end of the lake is a short .5-mile trail through lowlands and a Children's Forest. In spring 1990, children from the community and their families planted 600 trees as a major part of the reforestation effort. What a wonderful idea! Fifty years from now, those same children can bring their grandkids back to show them how they helped restore one small piece of their natural environment.

On the east side of the lake is a nature center with displays as well as a children's theater. Educational programs are offered year-round. East of the center is the Buzz N' Bloom Prairie containing close to 100 native prairie species. A trail through the prairie leads to a foot bridge

Bill Banks

Waterfall at Lake Katherine.

Lake Katherine Nature Preserve

Ridgeland Ave.

Bridge

N

Calumet-Sag Channel

Ridge

Navajo Creek

College Dr.

Sepa Waterfalls

Harlem Ave.

Bridge

Restrooms

Phone

Fountain

Environmental
Learning Center

Parking

Waterfall
Gardens
& Prairie

Rt. 83

75th Ave.

76th Ave.

N.& W. R.R.

Bridge

Children's
Forest

Tinley Creek
Trail Connection

Southwest Hwy.

Bridge

over a bubbling brook heading east to Harlem Avenue. An underpass at Harlem leads to the 33-acre Eastern Preserve with 2 miles of hiking trails through woods and prairie. After crossing under Harlem, you will encounter a massive waterfall flowing into the Cal-Sag Channel. Built by the Water Reclamation District of Greater Chicago, the falls at the Worth station naturally aerate the waters of the very slow moving channel, thus protecting the environment for fish and aquatic plants. One of five Sidestream Elevated Pool Aeration (SEPA) stations in the Chicago area, the Worth waterfalls really add to the enjoyment of the hike. You might also see a slow moving barge propelled eastward by a towboat heading to Calumet Harbor on Lake Michigan, the largest port on all the Great Lakes. Mississippi River barges get access to the Great Lakes and the East Coast via the Cal-Sag Channel and the Calumet River. Like its counterpart to the north, the Chicago Sanitary & Ship Canal, the Cal-Sag Channel was constructed between 1911 and 1922 to help control pollution of Chicago's drinking water by reversing the flow of the Calumet River so that it headed southwest rather than into Lake Michigan. Before then a stream ran through the area. Native Americans called it the Checagou just as they did the river to the north now called the Chicago River. In fact, some south-siders dispute the conventional wisdom that Jolliet and Marquette trekked up the Des Plaines River. Rather they argue that the river that once ran where the Cal-Sag Channel now flows was more navigable and thus the preferred route by Native Americans and the true route of the early French explorers.

The 2 miles of trail in the Eastern Preserve include a 1-mile wood-chip path paralleling the channel called the Old Canoe Path Trail. The original dredging of the channel as well as a major widening from 60 to 225 feet by the Army Corps of Engineers in 1955 left huge piles of earth and stone forming a long ridge paralleling the channel. Since then trees and plants have grown on the ridge. A 1-mile Overlook Trail serves to complete a loop back to the nature center. This trail is rugged in spots with loose stone and tree roots. Also the pathway was hard to find and follow due to overgrown vegetation. I would suggest that only those with sturdy shoes and strong legs try the Overlook Trail until planned improvements are completed.

Beaver, coyote, and fox have been spotted here as well as great horned owl, black-crowned-night heron, and many types of nesting birds. Bank swallows are being attracted to the area through the installation of clay tubes along the channel.

The trails are open for hiking only. A bike rack is available near the entrance by the community clubhouse. A drinking fountain, soft drinks, and restroom are available at the nature center. Grounds are open from dawn until 10 p.m. daily. Trails are open for cross-country skiing in winter. Call 708-361-1873 for more information.

Palos Preserves

Nestled in southwestern Cook County is Chicagoland's largest county forest preserve site. Visitors will discover lakes, ponds, forest, meadows, and sloughs throughout the 14,000-acre Palos Preserves. This is as close to wilderness as you can get in Chicagoland.

These preserves were formed by the last glacier that sculpted hills, canyons, and ravines leaving behind huge potholes from the melting ice to form lakes, ponds, and sloughs. Natural and man-made waterways border as well as intersect the preserves. The Des Plaines River, the Chicago Sanitary and Ship Canal, and the I&M Canal flow from the north part of the preserve southwest to the Illinois River. The Calumet-Sag Channel bisects the preserve and flows west to merge with the Chicago Sanitary and Ship Canal near the DuPage/Cook County border.

You'll discover 35 miles of unpaved, multi-use trails through the Palos Preserves as well as many miles of additional footpaths branching from the main trail. You could hike at Palos for a week and not cover every trail. The narrow footpaths are not open for biking or horseback riding. You'll also find 3 miles of hiking-only trails at the Little Red Schoolhouse Nature Center and 6.2 miles of trails for cross-country skiers and hikers at Camp Sagawau.

The boundless variety of ecosystems, flora, and fauna as well as the many places for solitary journeys and challenging hills make the Palos Preserves one of the best places for hiking and off-road bicycling in the NHC. And if you want to learn your trees, the Palos Preserves is where to do it! Sycamores and ironwood abound at McClaughry Springs. Pawpaw trees and shingle oaks can be found in PawPaw Woods. This is as far north as these native trees can survive. The woods of Palos are filled with towering white oaks, the state tree, as well as black and red oaks.

How to get there:

Given the enormous size and scope of the Palos Preserves, parking locations are innumerable. We will describe recommended places to park that provide easy trail access to the nature centers and the multi-use trails. (See map.) North of the Cal-Sag Channel, from the Willow Springs Road intersection with Archer Avenue (south of the Des Plaines River), take Willow Springs south of 95th Street. Here Willow Springs becomes 104th Avenue. Proceed south. The Little Red Schoolhouse Nature Center entrance is on the west side. You can access the multi-use trail south of the parking lot where it intersects with the nature center path leading to the White Oak Trail.

Little Red School House Nature Center

A century ago, Palos Hills farmers sent their children to school in a one-room log cabin near what is now the busy intersection of 95th Street and La Grange Road. Classes continued until 1948. Seven years later the Forest Preserve District of Cook County converted the building to a nature center. Inside, children of all ages can explore the world of nature up-close. In one area, busy bees perform intricate dances, spinning in circles, moving forward and back. These dances give exact directions to where other bees can find flowers producing nectar they need to make their honey. If you prefer snakes and snapping turtles, you can get close views of them inside the center as well.

Outside, more exhibits await you including a collection of 1880-vintage farm implements and interpretive signs providing a wealth of information on plants, animals, and ecosystems you will discover along the trails. One sign described mileage to nearby sites and those much farther away. For example, Lake Michigan is 16 miles from the preserve and the sun is 93 billion miles away. Luckily, the nature trails are a shorter distance. The .3-mile Farm Pond trail heads west from the center's rear leading to the 1.8-mile Black Oak trail. As you walk, look for the black oak's fallen acorns which have ragged-edged cups. Then look for a tree with deeply furrowed bark, toothed leaf lobes, and gray hairy buds. These native Illinois trees are rare, so enjoy them while you are here.

The Black Oak Trail winds on packed earth through wooded and hilly terrain and along the Long John Slough. In summer, you can enjoy the white flowers of the water lilies, a native species, covering much of the water's surface. In fall and spring, look for large numbers of waterfowl and shorebirds congregated on the slough. Near the shallow edges, you will find the dabbling ducks, such as a mallard that feeds by tipping up its body to reach down to snack on aquatic plants and seeds. In the deeper areas, look for diving ducks such as scaup that plunge into the water's depth to snatch aquatic insects, plants, and mollusks. You can identify a scaup by its blue bill with a dark point at the end, dark head and breast, golden-colored eye, and whitish body, with black rear.

South of the parking area you'll find the trailhead for the 1-mile White Oak Trail looping through white oaks. These trees have round-lobed leaves (as opposed to the black oak with its toothed leaves). The bark is only shallowly furrowed and gray, compared with the black oak's much darker bark. These hiking-only trails are a perfect place to take young children or for adults who want a short walk in the woods.

A water pump, bike rack, public phone, soda machine, and portable restrooms are available near the exhibit building. Nature walks and other programs are offered year-round. Call 708-839-6897.

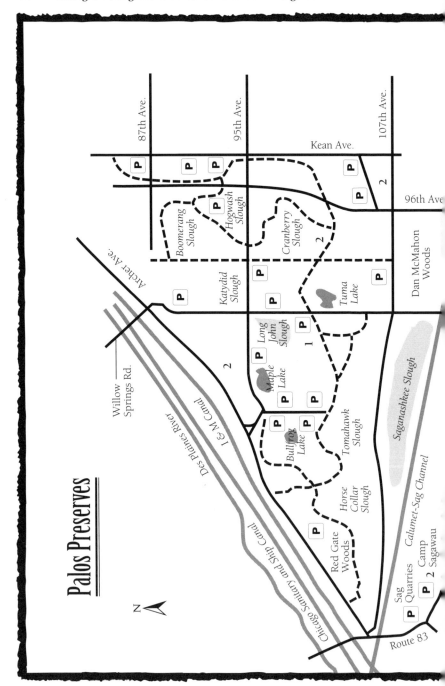

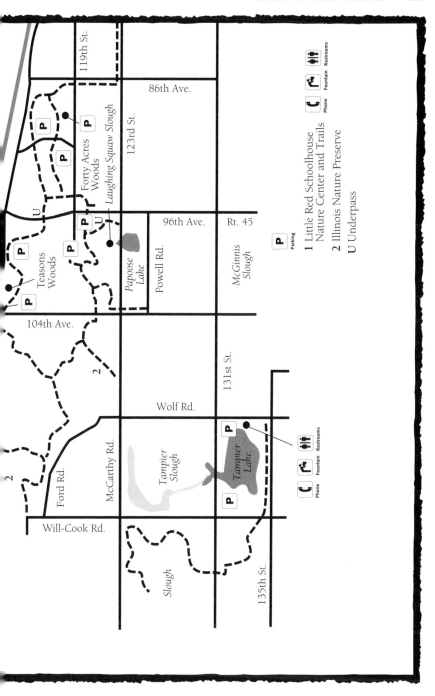

119th St.

86th Ave.

Forty Acres Woods

Laughing Squaw Slough

123rd St.

96th Ave.

Rt. 45

Powell Rd.

Papoose Lake

McGinnis Slough

Teasons Woods

104th Ave.

2

131st St.

Wolf Rd.

McCarthy Rd.

Tampier Slough

Tampier Lake

Ford Rd.

Will-Cook Rd.

Slough

135th St.

U

1 Little Red Schoolhouse
   Nature Center and Trails

2 Illinois Nature Preserve

   U Underpass

Phone   Fountain   Restrooms

Parking

Palos Multi-Use Trails/North of the Cal-Sag Channel

South of Archer Avenue and north of the Cal-Sag Channel is an 18-mile network of unpaved, multi-use trails with surfaces varying from packed earth to crushed limestone to cinder to gravel. The Forest Preserve District of Cook County plans to install a crushed limestone surface on all the multi-use trails here.

As you travel away from roads deeper into the forest, street noises fade into natural sounds. Chipmunks' piercing calls echo in the woods. Birds, especially in spring and early summer, sing as they flit from tree to tree. During spring migration, you'll enjoy a feast for the eyes. To stoke up for their long journey north to breed, colorful birds from the neotropics search for insects hiding in the trees' leaves. Bring your binoculars in May to enjoy some 30 kinds of warblers, tiny insect eaters with colorful patterns such as blue wings and yellow heads or black and red tails. Some will remain here to nest; others will fly farther north to Canada. Birds are attracted to water in spring and you may, for instance, discover a scarlet tanager with its deep red body and jet black wings, bathing in a creek on a warm spring day.

Forest Preserve District of Cook County

Toboggan slide at Swallow Cliff Woods.

The terrain is hilly and climbs are challenging. You will be rewarded with lovely views of creeks, woods, lakes, ponds, and sloughs. Daniel Webster describes a slough as "an abyss. . . a place of deep mud or mire." At the Palos Preserves, the sloughs are more aptly defined as lakes and ponds brimming with wildlife. Their names are captivating and picturesque: Saganashkee, Crawdad, Red Wing, and Belly Deep. The multi-use trails are open for hiking, bicycling, and horse riding. Be careful; you'll encounter many hilly areas with washouts as well as roots and rocks on the trail. The pathways are not well-marked, and you'll find many trail intersections, so bring a compass to avoid getting lost. You will eventually come out to a road or preserve picnic area where you can get your bearings. Water pumps, shelters, and rustic restrooms are located in most picnic areas near the trails.

For bicyclists, a mountain or hybrid bike is recommended to handle these trails effectively. Please stay on the 8-foot-wide maintained trails and don't venture off the path where you might disturb the fragile eco-system. The narrow foot paths are not open to equestrians or bicyclists.

Cross-country skiers will find 6.8 miles of trail open in winter near the Maple Lake area.

Sag Valley Multi-Use Trails

South of the Cal-Sag Channel, you will find 17 miles of unpaved, multi-use trail meandering through the hilly mature woodland areas.

How to get there:

Take Route 83 south to the Swallow Cliff Toboggan Slide entrance .2 mile west of 96th Avenue (Route 45).

Named for the bank swallows that nested in the cliffs here, Swallow Cliff Woods is a good place to start your trek through the secluded wilderness.

Recently, controversy has arisen regarding the impact of mountain biking on the natural areas at Palos and Deer Grove Preserves. Both areas have rugged, hilly terrain that attracts a growing number of mountain bikers. Unfortunately, some overzealous bicyclists have significantly damaged the vegetation in some sensitive natural areas, particularly the ravines. Consequently, at the time of writing, the narrow trails in the Swallow Cliff Woods area and throughout all the Palos Preserves have been closed to bicycling and horseback riding while restoration of the ravines and other areas is underway. The Forest Preserve District has installed signage that helps trail users know which trails are open to what type of use. Some 10 miles of crushed limestone surfaced trails in Swallow Cliff Woods are open for bicyclists. Partnering with trail user groups and environmental organizations, the Forest Preserve District intends to protect the sensitive natural areas of Palos while offering challenging trails that recognize the popularity of mountain biking.

When the snow falls, cross-country skiers will find 6.2 miles of groomed trails here. You can also rent toboggans and take a break in the warming shelter as well as use the heated restrooms.

Camp Sagawau

On the far west side of the Palos Preserves south of the Cal-Sag Channel you will find Camp Sagawau, open by reservation only. Here you can hike through Cook County's only natural rock canyon. Special programs include a canyon hike in which participants wade through a creek to enjoy the ferns, wildflowers, and rock formations. In spring, lush green ferns begin to unfold from closed fiddle-like branches to lacy green delights. Naturalists will also lead you on fossil hunts, and in the winter, you can participate in Nordic ski clinics. The camp is open for cross-country skiing when the snow base is sufficient. For more information on how to take a trip through this unique area call 630-257-2045.

How to get there:

Take Route 83 south of the Cal-Sag Channel and east of Archer Avenue. Route 83 is also 111th Street here. Proceed east for a short distance to the Camp Sagawau entrance on the north side of Route 83.

Tampier Lake Multi-Use Trail

You'll find another 4.5 miles of unpaved, multi-use trails south of McCarthy Road and west of Wolf Road near Tampier Lake and Tampier Slough.

Forest Preserve District of Cook County

Rock Canyon at Camp Sagawau.

How to get there:

Take Will-Cook Road south of McCarthy Road and 131st Street to the Tampier Lake entrance .1 mile south of 131st Street on the east side.

This multi-use trail is open for bicycling but is more suitable for mountain bikers as well as hikers. The .9-mile section south of Tampier Lake along 135th Street is relatively flat, bumpy, and not very interesting except for a nice view of the lake. The trail crosses Will-Cook Road and heads northwest through a large open field on a service road. North of 131st Street the trail becomes more interesting as it meanders through woods and open meadow before it dead ends at a slough. You can also rent rowboats at the boating center to get a different perspective of the lake.

The Palos Preserves provide trail users many unique adventures year-round. For the nature lover, there is no other place in Chicagoland that quite equals these preserves. So, enjoy and help protect these areas for future generations.

Cook County's I&M Canal Bicycle Trail and Arie Crown Forest Bicycle Trail

I&M Canal Bicycle Trail

Today you can hike and bike along the canal on the Forest Preserve District of Cook County's 8.9-mile I&M Canal Bicycle Trail near Willow Springs.

How to get there:

Take Route 83 or Willow Springs Road south of the Des Plaines River to Archer Avenue. Take Archer northwest of Willow Springs Road for .2 mile. Turn left at Market Street. Note the large bicycle trail welcome sign. Proceed through an industrial area for .2 mile. Cross under the Willow Springs Road bridge and over the Metra railroad tracks. Park in the first lot. The second is for Metra commuters.

The trail runs through the parking area heading northeast and southwest. A 2.3-mile linear central segment joins 3.3-mile loops at both ends. Heading northeast from the parking area, the asphalt trail leads through woods that

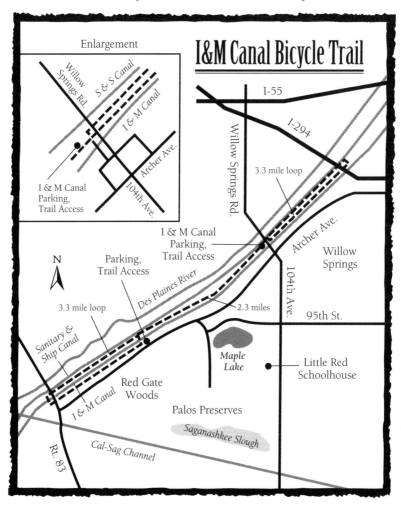

have grown since use of the canal was discontinued in 1933. The trail is shady and peaceful with little traffic sounds until you approach the I-294 underpass 1.6 miles out.

Just past the interstate, the trail turns back southwest paralleling the Chicago Sanitary and Ship Canal. This segment is 20-feet wide and is apparently used as a service road; although I have yet to see a vehicle on it. This northern section is a 3.3-mile loop.

Back at the trailhead, take the path to the southwest. Note how soil and vegetation have filled in the canal. Also note the remnants of an

I & M Canal near Willow Springs.

old stone bridge. Nature is slowly reclaiming man's developments. An intersection at 2.3 miles out from the trailhead is another 3.3-mile loop along the canal. Taking the path to the right you will pass two railroad crossings as well as an entrance road into a chemical company. The trail ends at the Route 83 overpass and loops back northeast to the trailhead. The two loops plus backtracking on the middle section make this an 11.2-mile round-trip.

At the time of writing, there was some bad news and there was some good news. The trail was temporarily closed near Route 83 so trail users had to backtrack rather than complete the loop. That's the bad news. The good news is that as part of a huge Route 83 bridge construction project, a trail connection has been established from the I&M Canal Bicycle Trail to the Centennial Trail currently under development (see Section 11). A pedestrian path with wire fence protection runs along the west side of the new Route 83 bridge. Bicyclists and hikers can now safely cross over the bridge. A scenic view of a huge auto scrap yard awaits you. But the trail connection will be much used and appreciated.

With no street crossings except for the one entrance road, and with the flat terrain, this is a good spot for beginning bicyclists or in-line skaters. The trail is clean and well-maintained as well as quiet and peaceful most of the way. At the trailhead, note the information display about the I&M Canal. There are no restrooms or water pumps along the trail; so come prepared.

Arie Crown Forest Bicycle Trail

South of Countryside, you'll find a 3.2-mile woodland trail through rolling terrain.

How to get there:

Take the Stevenson Expressway (I-55) to La Grange Road. Head north. There are two preserve entrances to your left. The first is .3 mile north of the Stevenson. An auto road loops through the preserve with trail access in several locations. Signposts near the parking areas identify the trail access points. Another entrance is also on La Grange north of 67th Street near Lake Ida. A third entrance is off Joliet Road (Route 66) west of La Grange Road. Take Brainard Road south into the preserve.

Most forest preserve-designated bicycle trails in Cook County have a paved asphalt surface. This trail is unpaved. Mostly packed earth, the trail is bumpy and narrow in spots. I did ride the trail uneventfully on my road bike. The Forest Preserve District of Cook County plans to install a crushed limestone surface. Until then, the trail is more suitable for mountain bikers. With several loops and trail intersections and no signage on the trail, it is easy to get lost, so bring a map and a compass. Since the auto road crosses the trail in several spots, you won't be lost long. There are a few hills to climb, a small creek to cross over, and nearby Lake Ida to enjoy. The northern portion is quiet and peaceful. Traffic sounds increase as you approach I-55 to the south.

The cross-county ski trail displayed on information signposts throughout the preserve is also the bicycle trail, unlike several other Cook County preserves where there are separate trails. Rustic restrooms, water pumps, and picnic tables are available near several of the parking areas.

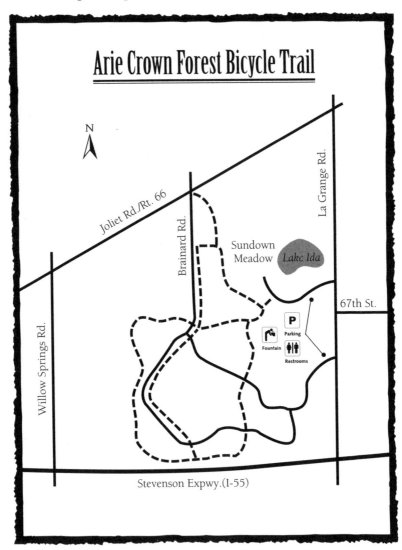

Arie Crown Forest Bicycle Trail

At the time of writing, the auto road through the preserve was temporarily closed at the Brainard Road and southern LaGrange Road entrances due to vandalism. Call the Forest Preserve District of Cook County on 708-771-1000 for more information.

Salt Creek Greenway

Salt Creek runs through northwestern Cook County, then flows south to DuPage County before heading back east into central Cook County where it empties into the Des Plaines River south of Brookfield. Much of the way, forest preserve greenways surround the stream. While you'll find no salt water here today, there is a story that the name Salt Creek came from a 19th century farmer's mishap. His wagon, loaded with salt barrels, got stuck in the water during a crossing. The next day he discovered the salt had washed into the creek, thus his misadventure lives on. By the 1970s, with all the development in the western suburbs, water quality had deteriorated badly. Thanks to more effective sewage treatment and the establishment of natural area greenways surrounding the creek, water quality is much improved today. As a result, waterfowl and other wildlife have returned. You'll find trails at three sites along the Salt Creek greenway in central Cook County.

Susan Van Horn

Hank Erdmann

Spring in Bemis Woods.

Bemis Woods

A 3-mile unpaved, multi-use trail runs through the gently rolling terrain along or near Salt Creek in the Bemis Woods Preserve north of Western Springs. The western trailhead for the Salt Creek Bicycle Trail is also here.

How to get there:

Take Ogden Avenue (Route 34) .5 mile east of the Tri-State Tollway

(I-294). The entrance is to the north. A second entrance is a bit farther east off of Wolf Road .6 mile north of Ogden. Both entrances have easy access to the multi-use trail. (See map.) The bicycle path trailhead is only accessible from the Ogden Avenue entrance as described below.

The multi-use trail loops through hilly woodlands and along a meandering creek. The surface is packed earth or loose gravel in some spots. The pathway is mostly 8-to-10-foot wide but narrows to a single track overgrown with vegetation in some spots. It's easy to lose your way with all the trail intersections, so bring a compass and map. This trail is open to hikers, equestrians, and bicyclists. It offers a bit more rugged alternative to the nearby asphalt trail. A mountain or hybrid bike will more effectively handle the roots, stumps, and washouts on the dirt pathways.

Salt Creek Bicycle Trail

The 6.6-mile paved asphalt path runs from Bemis Woods to Brookfield Zoo passing through or near the communities of Western Springs, La Grange, La Grange Park, North Riverside, Westchester, and finally Brookfield.

How to get there:

The western trailhead is in Bemis Woods Preserve off Ogden Avenue as described above. Trail access is south of the toboggan slide. The eastern trailhead is at Brookfield Woods Preserve northwest of Brookfield Zoo. Take 31st Street west of Des Plaines Avenue and east of La Grange Road (Routes 45/12/20). Parking is also available in the Brezina Woods Preserve off Mannheim Road. (See map.)

On an early May ride, wildflowers carpeted the woods along the path. The trail is curvy and has some hills. There are five road crossings and several forest preserves along the way. At 1.6 miles out from the Bemis Woods trailhead, you will come to a trail intersection with the LaGrange Park Bicycle Path. A short (.2-mile) spur heads right to a residential neighborhood at Brainard and Jackson Streets in LaGrange Park. While the sidetrip is a short one, it is worth taking. A new trail bridge across Salt Creek offers a scenic view with tree branches

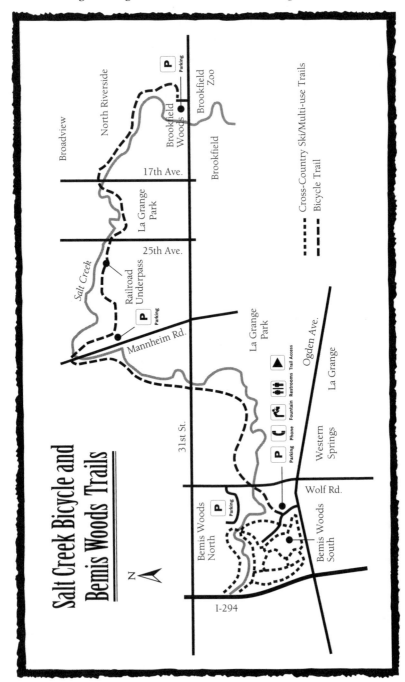

Salt Creek Bicycle and Bemis Woods Trails

overhanging the creek. Narrow side trails head off along the creek and into the woods. Hugging the creek in spots sometimes along small bluffs, the trail runs mostly through mature woodlands. A prairie restoration is underway north of the zoo.

Be particularly cautious at the five street crossings! You'll encounter extremely heavy traffic at several crossings, especially, La Grange Road. High curbs and no stoplights at some streets contribute to your need for attention. Also there is a very steep downhill heading west at the Wolf Road crossing. A caution sign is needed here. Go slowly! I really enjoy this trail, but would not recommend bringing young children just learning to ride. Bridges or stoplights with a push-to-walk button would really be helpful at the Wolf Road, 31st Street, and 17th Avenue crossings.

You will find water pumps as well as rustic and modern restrooms, picnic tables, and shelters in the forest preserve picnic areas along the way. However, I couldn't find a water pump at the eastern trailhead in Brookfield Woods.

If you haven't encountered enough wildlife on the trail, head east on 31st Street .2 mile from the eastern trailhead at Brookfield Woods to tropical rain forests and African grasslands. The Forest Preserve District of Cook County owns and the Chicago Zoological Society operates the world-famous Brookfield Zoo. Here you can observe more than 2,500 animals of 400 different species and enjoy a relaxing walk. Call 708-485-0263 for hours and admission prices.

Wolf Road Prairie

Approximately eighty acres of oak savanna, prairie, and marsh thrive in this Illinois Nature Preserve in Westchester. The Depression helped to save the land, which had been planned for residential development in the 1920s, in its natural state. Also the wetlands here made the area ill-suited for growing crops or grazing animals. As a result, at Wolf Road Prairie, you can walk through land that is much like the first settlers encountered 160 years ago. Recognized as the finest and largest silt loam soil prairie east of the Mississippi River, Wolf Road Prairie is incredibly diverse. Over 320 plant species flourish here.

Hank Erdmann

Wolf Road Prairie in summer.

How to get there:

Take Ogden Avenue east of I-294 past Bemis Woods Forest Preserve to Wolf Road. Head north on Wolf to 31st Street. Head west (left) on 31st for .1 mile. There are three small concrete parking area pull-ins north of 31st Street. Park in the middle one. Here you can pick up an excellent trail guide at the information signpost.

The pathway near the entrance is a set of rectangular grids of concrete connected with narrow earthen footpaths. The concrete walkways are old sidewalks installed in the 1920s for a proposed residential development that never happened. Take the path to the right of the information signpost where you'll find a 250-year-old bur oak tree. This specimen is a perfect example of its species which, thanks to a thick, resilient bark survived the frequent fires that swept through and rejuvenated the prairie.

Smaller brethren surround the giant tree in an oak savanna, perhaps the rarest ecosystem in the world. Growing beneath the trademark bur oak in this combination forest/grassland are plants such as rue anemones and wild hyacinths. In fall, the lovely woodland sunflower brightens the shady oaks with its yellow-hued petals.

The prairie blooms May through October. The trail guide describes what you will encounter such as muskrats, blue-winged teals, and other animals.

Valerie Spale and Phil Cihlar, volunteers in the Save the Prairie Society, gave me a tour of the prairie one hot day in late July. Having left my burnt-out lawn at home, I was struck by the vibrancy, color, and diversity that abounds in the summer heat. They pointed out prairie dock, yellow coneflowers, rattlesnake master, Indian grass, and myriad other forbs. Every few weeks different plants bloom and predominate. Ongoing burns and removal of alien plants keep the prairie thriving.

If you walk all the concrete sidewalks and then out to the prairie house at the far northern section of the preserve, you will have a 2-mile hike. The prairie house has an interesting history and future. The German settlers in a small community called Franzosenbusch erected a two-room schoolhouse in 1852. Plans are to restore the original structure with a new role as a nature center. Once again, it will be a schoolhouse.

To protect the prairie plants, the path is open to hikers only. You can lock your bike at the signpost. Be sure to wear long pants. In summer and early fall, the trails can be overgrown with vegetation. Also, many of the concrete slabs have cracks and become uneven, so watch your step.

You'll find no facilities here, so bring water on hot days. Several fast-food restaurants are east of Wolf Road along 31st Street. The Wolf Road Prairie is preserved by a consortium consisting of an active volunteer group called Save the Prairie Society, the Illinois Department of Natural Resources, the Forest Preserve District of Cook County, and the Illinois Nature Preserves Commission.

Monthly Ecotours and special events are held throughout the year covering various conservation topics. Call 708-865-8736 for more information.

Navy Pier/Chicago River Walks

The symbolic starting point for a trek through the NHC can be found in downtown Chicago at Navy Pier. As you head out toward the pier on Illinois Street, near the fountain in Gateway Park, three colorful sculpted benches welcome you. As you get closer, you will find the works of art are mosaic covered benches composed of ceramic and glass tiles affixed to curving black concrete. Over 350 people were involved in this complicated and beautiful community art project that portrays life along the I&M Canal in the 19th century as well as underwater scenes.

How to get there:

On foot or bike, take the 18.5-mile Chicago Park District Bikeway that runs along Lake Michigan's Shore. Navy Pier offers great views of Lake Michigan and the Chicago Skyline. By motor vehicle take Lake Shore Drive, north of the loop to Illinois Street. Head east on Illinois to the parking area at Navy Pier.

Street musicians, restaurants, a huge Ferris wheel, a carousel, tour boats, and many other amusements create a peaceful oasis amid the hustle and bustle of the city. Plenty of bike racks are available. Farther west new housing developments are springing up along the north and south branches of the Chicago River. Plans call for an extended river walk with benches, street lights, and landscaped terraces.

When Fort Dearborn was built in 1803, the Chicago River flowed into Lake Michigan a short distance south of what today is Navy Pier. Fed by northern and southern branches that converge at Wolf Point (near the Merchandise Mart) the river headed east for one mile along present day Wacker Drive.

Walking on the sidewalk along Wacker Drive toward Navy Pier, it is a bit difficult to understand how this rather narrow river, that is dyed green each Saint Patrick's Day, could have been the gateway that opened up the main transportation route from the East Coast to the Upper Midwest 150 years ago. As Chicago grew, more and more raw sewage and polluted liquids were conveniently dumped in the river, which then transported the awful mess into Lake Michigan. Since Chicago water comes from Lake Michigan, the citizenry received part of the polluted liquids back in the form of drinking water. Not a very good arrangement! In January 1900, the problem was solved (at least from Chicago's point of view) by the opening of the 28-mile Chicago Sanitary and Ship Canal which reversed the flow of the Chicago River.

The Friends of the Chicago River have produced a series of five walking-tour brochures for the Chicago River Trail along or near the waterway: the Downtown Section, a Near North Branch Section (from the Waterfall at Foster Avenue to Goose Island at Chicago Avenue), the North Branch Section (from the waterfall at Foster Avenue upstream to the Chicago city limits), the South Branch Section (from Roosevelt Road to Damen Avenue), and the section along the Chicago Sanitary and Ship Canal (from Damen Avenue to Chicago Portage Woods at Harlem Avenue). Each brochure contains a map detailing a walking route for that section as well as loads of historical information and items of interest along the river.

Call the Friends of the Chicago River at 312-939-0490 for more information about the walking tours and how to get the maps. The Friends organization is a not-for-profit agency working to protect and restore the waterway. Their vision is "a river where nature and people coexist."

Greenway Interconnecting Trails

For the beginner hiker or biker, 1, 2, or 5-mile trails are sufficient for getting exercise while enjoying nature. But over time many of us want to push on to adventures of longer distances over different paths and trails.

In Will County, the rest of Chicagoland, and nationwide, significant progress is being made to interconnect existing park, forest preserve, and other trails. The term greenway identifies a corridor of open land such as an old railroad or utility right-of-way or a waterway that can provide transportation for people and/or wildlife while restoring or preserving the natural environment. Often the greenway contains a trail. The I&M Canal right-of-way, the Kankakee River State Park, and the Old Plank Road Trail described in this guidebook are all examples of greenways.

Greenways preserve and protect water and air quality and animal life as well as provide recreational opportunities and self-propelled commuting. The Chicagoland greenway system is viewed by many to be the most extensive of any metropolitan area in the country. Greenway initiatives in other metropolitan areas have also been successful in linking existing parks, forests, and trails. Given the high cost of land acquisition and the scarcity of available public funds, greenways are also proving to be the most cost-effective way to provide access to open space.

You may be able to use a greenway trail to visit a park or forest preserve on your bike rather than in your car. These linear park trails are typically much safer than the highways since contending with horses or bicycles is less risky than dealing with cars, buses, and trucks. The purpose of this section is to describe some of the activities underway to provide significantly more trails in the near future within the NHC and Will County and to interconnect with trails originating in the surrounding counties and beyond.

The Northeastern Illinois Planning Commission (NIPC) is partnering with the Openlands Project to coordinate the planning for an interconnected set of trails that will soon cover 1,000 miles over the six-county Chicago area. Already 500 miles of such regional greenways exist. Linking these trail systems provides an increasingly interconnected network of trails similar to our highway and railroad systems.

The Northeastern Illinois Regional Greenways Plan was released in May 1993, with this purpose: "The Greenways Plan creates a vision of an interconnected region wide network of linear open spaces that will provide benefits to northeastern Illinois—environmental, recreational, economic, aesthetic, and even transportation via trails or waterways." The plan encompasses Cook, DuPage, Kane, Lake, McHenry, and Will Counties. Greenway opportunities and priorities for development are included in the plan. The existing greenway network provides an excellent starting point including the major waterways (Chicago, Des Plaines, DuPage, Fox, and Kankakee Rivers), the Lake Michigan shoreline, old railroad routes (such as the Illinois Prairie Path, and the Great Western Trails in Kane and DuPage Counties), and, of course, the Chicagoland portion of the Illinois & Michigan Canal National Heritage Corridor described in this book.

Will County and NHC Initiatives

- The 5.5-mile extension of the I&M Canal State Trail from Brandon Road Lock and Dam near Joliet to I-55.
- Completion of 3.7 miles of trails through the Joliet Iron Works Historic Site (under construction at the time of writing).
- Extension of the Rock Run Greenway.

Top priorities still in the planning stage are as follows:

- An 8-mile extension west of the Old Plank Road Trail from Mokena to Joliet.
- Construction of a 10-mile trail on the old Chicago, Milwaukee, and St. Paul Railroad right-of-way from Joliet to the Midewin National Tallgrass Prairie.
- Development of a trail system within Midewin.

Other potential new Will County trails include the following:

- DuPage River greenway trails through the communities of Naperville, Plainfield, Bolingbrook, Shorewood, and Channahon.
- A bikeway along the proposed I-355 extension.
- A trail from the Kankakee River near Custer Park to Midewin on an abandoned railroad right-of-way.
- Extension of the Virgil Gilman Trail through Plainfield south to Joliet and northeast to connect with the DuPage River Greenway.
- A network of trails in Channahon connecting to the I&M Canal State Trail.

Greenways Involvement

Many agencies are planning and implementing greenway trails. These include the City of Joliet, the Forest Preserve District of Will County, the U.S. Forest Service, Plainfield Township Park District, the Village of Lemont, and the Illinois Department of Natural Resources.

The Regional Greenways plan provides an excellent vision and framework, but many government agencies, private sector corporations, land-owners, and interested individuals must play a role in making the plan work. Voice your areas of interest if you'd like to be

I&M Canal State Trail in Winter.

involved in making the Chicagoland greenways network happen. For more information call NIPC at 312-454-0400 and/or Openlands Project at 312-427-4256.

Interconnecting Trails in Nearby Counties

Greenway trails in nearby counties offer opportunities for extended bike rides and hikes. Proposed trails in nearby counties will form an ever expanding network of off-road pathways. Some examples include the following:

• Old Plank Road Trail connections in Cook County to the Forest Preserve District's Tinley Creek and Thorn Creek Bicycle Trails.

• A Salt Creek Greenway trail along the creek through Cook and DuPage Counties much of the way from the Ned Brown Preserve in Schaumburg to the Chicago Portage site in Lyons.

• Completion of the 65-mile Des Plaines River Trail in Lake and Cook Counties from the Wisconsin border south to the Chicago Portage site. Most of the trail is already in place.

Jill Bergstrom, Courtesy Illinois Department of Natural Resources

Beyond Chicagoland

In the introduction to his book, *Greenways for America*, Charles E. Little describes the greenway initiatives as a "remarkable citizen-led movement to get us out of our cars and into the landscape—on paths and trails through corridors of green that can link city to country and people to nature from one end of America to the other." Little describes examples both new and old from the Big Sur in California to the Illinois & Michigan Canal National Heritage Corridor to the Hudson River Valley Greenway in New York.

The National Park Service, the American Hiking Society, and a coalition of individuals and trail organizations are partnering in an effort called "Trails for All Americans—The National Trails Agenda Project." This effort began in 1988 when the President's Commission on American Outdoors recommended the development of a nation-wide network of hiking trails, bikeways, and bridle paths. Similar to the U.S. Interstate Highway System, planners envision backbone interstate trails interconnecting with state, county, and local community pathways. The goal is that most Americans would live within 15 minutes of a path that could access this national network.

Eight National Scenic and nine Historic Trails currently provide the major backbone network. For example, the Appalachian National Scenic Trail—a completed 2,144-mile trail through the Appalachian Mountains from Katahdin, Maine to Springer Mountain, Georgia.

While no National Scenic or Historic Trail runs through Will County, a major effort is underway to complete the 500+ mile Grand Illinois Trail that will run through Chicagoland, then head west to the Mississippi River, north to Galena, and back to Chicago. The Grand Illinois connects with the partially completed 6,300 mile American Discovery Trail.

The Grand Illinois Trail

So you say you want to take a really long hike or bike ride! The Illinois Department of Natural Resources is partnering with many other agencies and organizations to develop one nearby. The Grand Illinois Trail consists of a 475-mile circular loop from Navy Pier in Chicago past Starved Rock State Park to the Mississippi River via the

The Grand Illinois Trail

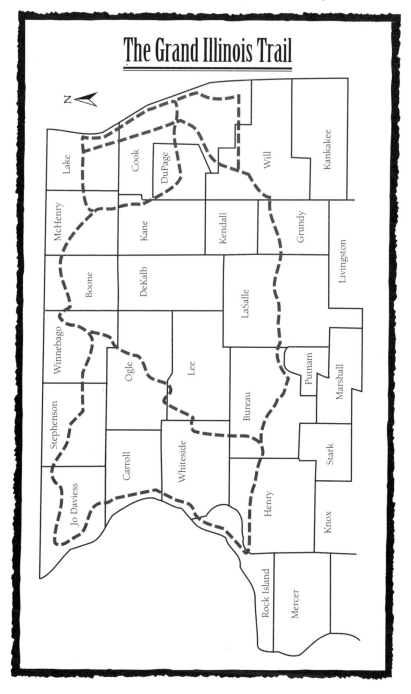

162 • *Hiking & Biking The I&M Canal National Heritage Corridor*

I&M Canal State Trail, the Kaskaskia/Alliance Trail and the Hennepin Canal State Trail. The trail then heads north along the Great River Trail to Savanna and Mississippi Palisades State Park, continues along The Northwest Hills Trail in Jo Daviess County to Galena then returns to Chicago through the other counties bordering Wisconsin.

In total, the Grand Illinois Trail system will contain 500+ miles of rail trails, bike paths, canal tow paths, and greenways along with street routes and lightly traveled township and county roads as it traverses the state. Camping and lodging is available along the way. Hikers, bicyclists, equestrians and other trail users will be able to see parts of the state they probably have never visited before. Trail enthusiasts will be able to enjoy nearby adventure vacations taking on the entire trail in a single effort or more likely completing one segment at a time.

Existing trails described in this guidebook are part of the Grand Illinois: the I&M Canal State Trail in Will, Grundy, and LaSalle Counties, the Old Plank Road Trail in Cook and Will Counties, and the partially completed Centennial Trail. Additional trail opportunities relating to the Grand Illinois Trail will include parts of the existing Fox River Trail, the Illinois Prairie Path, the Prairie Trail, the Des Plaines River and Green Bay Trails in Lake and Cook Counties, the Chicago Lakefront Path, and other existing and proposed on-and off-road routes..

In fact, approximately 250 miles of trail are already in place. Projects totaling 40 miles are funded for construction or improvement. The 15.1-mile Kaskaskia/Alliance Trail and the 59-mile Hennepin Canal Trail are currently under development with trail already open on the Hennepin. In addition, at least for now, about 185 miles are proposed along designated local roads or streets. The goal is to complete the Grand Illinois Trail by the year 2000. While it will take time and a major effort by the involved agencies to construct, the Grand Illinois Trail will be an outstanding asset to trail users as well as the communities along the way. If you are interested in finding out more, call the Grand Illinois Trail Coordinator at 815-732-9072 or the IDNR Division of Planning at 815-782-3715.

The Grand Illinois will connect with a new national path system, also under development, the American Discovery Trail.

American Discovery Trail

The American Discovery Trail Society and many other agencies and organizations are partnering in the development of the 6,300-mile American Discovery Trail (ADT). Three thousand five hundred miles of trails consisting of both on-and off-road routes are already marked. From the trailhead near the Atlantic Ocean at the Cape Henlopen State Park in Delaware to the Pacific Ocean at the Point Reyes National Seashore in California, the ADT will run through urban and remote areas in 15 states and Washington D.C. Through the midwestern states including Illinois, there will be both a northern and a southern route forming a gigantic 3,500-mile loop from Cincinnati to Denver. Open to hikers, bicyclists, and equestrians, the ADT will connect to six national scenic trails and ten national historic trails as well as many regional and local trail systems such as ours here in Chicagoland. In northern Illinois, the ADT coexists with a portion of the Grand Illinois Trail which includes the I&M Canal State Trail and the Old Plank Road Trail described in this guidebook as well as the Kaskaskia/Alliance Trail and the Hennepin Canal State Trail. Trail users will truly be able to sample the diversity of America from the seashores to the deserts, to the mountains to the prairies, to the rivers and streams, to the towns and cities along the way. Contact the American Discovery Trail Society at 800-663-2387 (national) or 630-985-3895 (local) for more information.

Watch for Grand Illinois and ADT trail markers as you hike and bike the Old Plank Road Trail and the I&M Canal State Trail.

Trail User Support

Unfortunately, recent federal budget cutting initiatives in Washington have negatively impacted the progress of trails development. Some of the planned trail systems mentioned above will be delayed or perhaps never built. If you are interested in seeing the expansion of trails and off-road hiking and bicycling paths, voice your opinions to local, state, and federal government representatives, particularly your U.S. House of Representatives legislators.

Appendices

Illinois & Michigan Canal National Heritage Corridor
visitor centers and lodging are listed on pages 165 to 167.

I&M Canal National Heritage Corridor Visitor Centers

I&M Canal NHC Commission Office
15701 S. Independence Blvd.
Lockport, IL 60441-6584
815-740-2047

Little Red Schoolhouse Nature Center
9800 S. 104th Ave.
Willow Springs, IL 60480
708-839-6897

Isle a la Cache Museum
501 E. Romeo Road
Romeoville, IL 60446
815-886-1467

I&M Canal Visitor Center
The Gaylord Building
200 W. Eighth St.
Lockport, IL 60441
815-838-4830

Will County Historical Society Museum
803 S. State St.
Lockport, IL 60441
815-838-5080

Will-Joliet Bicentennial Park
201 W. Jefferson St.
Joliet, IL 60435
815-740-2216

I&M Canal State Trail-Channahon Access
P. O. Box 54, 2 W. Story St.
Channahon, IL 60410
815-476-4271

I&M Canal State Trail-
Gebhard Woods Access
102 Ottawa St.
Morris, IL 60450
815-942-0796

Goose Lake Prairie State Natural Area
5010 N. Jugtown Road
Morris, IL 60450
815-942-2899

Buffalo Rock State Park Information Center
Ottawa, IL 61350
815-433-2224

Illinois Waterway Visitor Center
Rt. 1, Dee Bennett Road
Ottawa, IL 61350
815-667-4054

Starved Rock State Park Visitor Center
Utica, IL 61373
815-667-4906

Heritage Corridor Visitors Bureau
Joliet Office
81 N. Chicago St.
Joliet, IL 60432
815-727-2323 or 1-800-926-2262

Utica Office
723 S. Clark St.
Utica, IL 61373
815-667-4356

Willow Springs Office
8695 Archer Avenue
Willow Springs, IL 60480
708-839-1322

Lodging

Cook County

Super 8
7887 W. 79th Street
Bridgeview 708-458-8008

Hampton Inn
6251 Joliet Road
Countryside 708-354-5200

J.C. Countryside Motel
Joliet Road
Countryside 708-352-3113

LaGrange Motel
5846 S. LaGrange Road
Countryside 708-352-5640

William Tell Holiday Inn
6201 Joliet Road
Countryside 708-354-4200

Wishing Well Motel
Joliet Road & Brainard Avenue
Countryside 708-352-3615

Best Western Inn
5631 S. LaGrange Road
LaGrange 708-352-2480

Budget Host
8640 Ogden
Lyons 708-447-6363

Chicagoland Motel
7225 Ogden
Lyons 708-447-7910

Plank Towers Motel
7307 Ogden
Lyons 708-442-5120

Presidential Inn
3922 S. Harlem Avenue
Lyons 708-447-2890

Grundy County

Comfort Inn
70 W. Gore Road
Morris 815-942-1433

Holiday Inn Morris
I-80 at Rte. 47
Morris 815-942-6600

Park Motel
1923 N. Division
Morris 815-942-1321

Super 8
70 Green Acres Drive
Morris 815-942-3200

LaSalle County

Days Inn
I-80 & Rte. 251
LaSalle 815-224-1060

Howard Johnson
Rte. 251 & I-80
LaSalle 815-224-2500

Kensington-Kaskaskia
217 Marquette Street
LaSalle 815-223-1200

Annie Tique's
Bed & Breakfast
378 Main Street
Marseilles 815-795-5848

Prairie Lake Lodge
2550 N. 32nd Road
Marseilles 815-795-5107

Elizabeth's Bed & Breakfast
1100 5th Street
Mendota 815-539-5555

Lord Stocking's
Bed & Breakfast
803 3rd Avenue
Mendota 815-539-7905

Super 8
508 Highway 34E
Mendota 815-539-7429

Brightwood Inn
2704 N. IL Rte. 178
Ogelsby 815-667-4600

Days Inn
120 N. Lewis Avenue
Ogelsby 815-883-9600

Holiday Inn Express
900 Holiday Blvd.
Ogelsby 815-883-3535

Comfort Inn
510 E. Etna Road
Ottawa 815-433-9600

Holiday Inn Express
120 W/ Stevenson Road
Ottawa 815-883-3535

Marcia's Bed & Breakfast
3003 N. IL Rte. 71
Ottawa 815-434-5217

Ottawa Inn
I-80 at Rte. 23
Ottawa 815-434-3400

Sands Motel
1215 LaSalle Street
Ottawa 815-434-6440

Super 8 Motel
I-80, Rte. 23 Etna Road
Ottawa 815-434-2888

Surrey Motel
Rte. 23 & I-80
Ottawa 815-433-1263

Comfort Inn Peru
5240 Trompeter Road
Peru 815-223-8585

Fairfield Inn Peru
4385 Venture Drive
Peru 815-223-7458

Motel 6
1900 May Road
Peru 815-224-2785

Super 8
1851 May Road
Peru 815-223-1848

Pine Towers Motel
Rte. 23N
Streator 815-672-3168

Town & Country Inn
2110 N. Bloomington
Streator 815-672-3183

Kishauwau on the Vermilion
Route 1
Tonica 815-442-8453

Landers House
115 E. Church Street
Utica 815-667-5170

Starved Rock Gateway Motel
Rt. 6 & 178
Utica 815-667-4238

Starved Rock Lodge &
Conference Center
P.O. Box 247
Utica 815-667-4211

Will County

Comfort Inn Bolingbrook
225 W.S. Frontage Road
Bolingbrook 630-226-0000

Holiday Inn Hotel & Suites
205 Remington Blvd.
Bolingbrook 630-679-1600

Ramada Limited
520 S. Bolingbrook Drive
Bolingbrook 630-972-9797

Manor Motel
I-55 & Rte. 6
Channahon 815-467-5385

Super 8 Motel
14 E. Northbrook Drive
Dwight 815-584-1888

Comfort Inn North
3235 Norman Avenue
Joliet 815-436-5141

Comfort Inn South
135 S. Larkin Avenue
Joliet 815-744-1770

Elks Motel
270 S.E. Frontage Road
Joliet 815-725-0101

Empress Hotel
2300 Empress Drive
Joliet 815-744-9400

Fairfield Inn North
3239 Norman Avenue
Joliet 815-436-6577

Fairfield Inn South
1501 River Boat Center
Drive
Joliet 815-741-3499

Fireside Resort
4200 W. Jefferson Street
Joliet 815-725-0111

Hampton Inn North
3555 Mall Loop Drive
Joliet 815-439-9500

Hampton Inn South
1521 Riverboat Center Drive
Joliet 815-725-2424

Holiday Inn Express
411 S. Larkin Avenue
Joliet 815-729-2000

Motel 6
1850 McDonough Street
Joliet 815-729-2800

Motel 6
3551 Mall Loop Drive
Joliet 815-439-1332

Ramada Limited
3231 Norman Drive
Joliet 815-439-4200

Ramada Limited
1520 Commerce Lane
Joliet 815-730-1111

Red Roof Inn
1750 McDonough Street
Joliet 815-741-2304

Super 8 Motel
1730 McDonough Street
Joliet 815-725-8855

Super 8
3401 Mall Loop Drive
Joliet 815-439-3838

Wingate Hotel
McDonald Drive
Joliet 815-741-2100

Oak Dell Bed & Breakfast
14505 W. 143rd Street
Lockport 708-301-0543

Super 8
9485 W. 191st Street
Mokena 708-479-7808

Country Host Motel
Monee-Manhattan Road
at I-57
Monee 708-534-2150

Country Inn & Suites
1265 Lakeview Drive
Romeoville 630-378-1052

Howard Johnson Express
Inn
1235 Lakeview Drive
Romeoville 630-226-1900

Super 8
1301 Marquette
Romoeville 630-759-8880

Days Inn
19747 Frontage Road
Shorewood 815-725-2180

HoJo Inn
24001 Lorenzo Road
Wilmington 815-476-4271

Van Duynes Motel
107 Bridge Street
Wilmington 815-476-2801

Nearby Bike Shops

You will find bike shops conveniently located near many of the trails and bike paths described in this guidebook.

Cook County

Alsip Bicycles
11600 South Pulaski Avenue
Alsip
708-371-8070

Morello's Bike Village
8827 West Ogden Avenue
Brookfield
708-485-6569

The Wheel Thing
15 South LaGrange Road
LaGrange
708-352-3822

Orland Park Schwinn Cyclery
14445 S. John Humphrey Drive
Orland Park
708-460-2999

Bicycle & Fitness
11933 South Harlem Avenue
Palos Heights
708-448-4601

DuPage County

Bikeline of Darien
2137 75th Street
Darien
630-769-5597

Blazing Saddles
888 75th Street
Willowbrook
630-986-2453

Grundy County

Grand Schwinn Cyclery
711 Liberty Street
Morris
815-942-1510

J & J Cyclery
350 Third Avenue
South Wilmington
815-237-2271

LaSalle County

Smitty's Bike Shop
1410 Guion Street
Ottawa
815-434-0717

Tullio's Big Dog Cyclery
525 1st Street
LaSalle
815-223-1776

Will County

Becvars Bikes
123 East 9th Street
Lockport
815-838-8836

Dave's Bikes Etc.
1416 North Broadway Street
Joliet
815-723-2204

Don's Bike Shop
25940 South Egyptian Trail
Monee
708-534-2453

Pedal Power Cyclery
1831 Constitution Road
New Lenox
815-485-7188

Sumbaum Cycle Company
114 North Larkin Avenue
Joliet
815-744-5333

Ski & Bike Chalet
R.R. 5
Shorewood
815-741-4456

Information provided by the Chicago Area Bicycle Dealers Association

Calendar of Events

Each event is shown under the month scheduled at time of publication. Call for more specific information.

January

Lake Katherine Winter Festival
Lake Katherine Nature Preserve,
Palos Heights
708-361-1873

Musher Mania
Monee Reservoir, Monee
Forest Preserve District of Will County
815-727-8700

Recycle the Christmas Spirit
Forest Preserve District of Will County
815-727-8700

Winter Feeding is for the Birds
Forest Preserve District of Will County
815-727-8700

Winter Festival
Swallow Cliff, Palos Park
The Forest Preserve District of Cook County
708-771-1014 or 708-771-1062

Winter Wilderness Weekend
Starved Rock State Park
815-667-4906

February

Cross-Country Ski Weekend
Matthiessen State Park
815-667-4906

Midwest Bicycle Show, Rosemont
847-202-0795

March

Earth Walk
Forest Preserve District of Will County
815-727-8700

April

Beginners & Intermediate Fishing Clinic
(April–September)
Monee Reservoir, Monee
Forest Preserve District of Will County
815-727-8700

Earth Day Event
Little Red Schoolhouse Nature Center
Palos Preserves, Willow Springs
The Forest Preserve District of Cook County
708-839-6897

Folks on Spokes Easter Ride
Governors State University, University Park
708-730-5179

Lake Katherine Arbor Day Celebration
Lake Katherine Nature Preserve,
Palos Heights
708-361-1873

Will County Folk Art Festival
Pioneer Settlement, Lockport
815-838-5080

Wildflower Walks (April–May)
Forest Preserve District of Will County
815-727-8700

May

Annual Wildflower Pilgrimage
Starved Rock State Park
815-667-4906

Bike to Work Week
Chicagoland Bicycle Federation
312-42-PEDAL

Cabin Fest
Goose Lake Prairie State Natural Area
Morris
815-942-2899

Earth Fair
Plum Creek Nature Center, Beecher
Forest Preserve District of Will County
815-727-8700

Lake Renwick Heron Rookery: Bird Viewing
& Interpretive Program (May–August),
Plainfield
Forest Preserve District of Will County
815-727-8700

Urban Adventures
Guided biking, boat, canoe, and walking
tours along the Chicago River
(May–October), Chicago
Friends of the Chicago River
312-361-1873

Wildflower Weekends
Pilcher Park, Joliet
815-741-7277

Wild Foods Workshop
Environmental Learning Center, Mokena
Forest Preserve District of Will County
815-727-8700

June

Annual Kankakee River Clean-up
Kankakee River State Park, Bourbonnais
815-933-1383

Environmental Awareness Expo
Little Red Schoolhouse Nature Center
Willow Springs
The Forest Preserve District of Cook County
708-839-6897

Family Camping Weekend
Plum Creek Nature Center, Beecher
Forest Preserve District of Will County
815-727-8700

Island Rendezvous
Isle a la Cache Museum, Romeoville
Forest Preserve District of Will County
815-727-8700

Montreal Canoe Weekend
Starved Rock State Park
815-667-4906

Old Canal Days Festival
Downtown Lockport
815-838-4744

July

A Gathering on the Theatiki
(French-Indian War Re-enactment)
Kankakee River State Park, Bourbonnais
815-933-1383

Dulcimer Festival
Gebhard Woods State Park
Illinois Department of Natural Resources
815-942-0796

Joliet Waterway Daze
Will-Joliet Bicentennial Park, Joliet
815-740-2216

Ottawa Riverfest Celebration
Downtown Ottawa
815-434-2737

Plainfield 4th of July Ride 30/60M
Joliet Bicycle Club
815-476-2044

August

Channahon Three Rivers Festival
Central Park, Channahon
815-467-7275

Morris Air Show
Morris Airport, Route 47
815-942-1600

Starved Rock Lock and Dam Tours
Illinois Waterway Visitors Center, Utica
815-667-4054

Sweet Corn Festival
Route 34 & Illinois Avenue, Mendota
815-539-6507

Utica Ambulance Porkfest
Memorial Park, Utica
815-667-4356

September

I&M Canal Rendezvous
Columbia Woods Forest Preserve,
Willow Springs
The Forest Preserve District of Cook County
708-352-4110

Lockport Civil War Days
Dellwood Park, Lockport
815-838-1183

Monarch Butterfly Festival
Lake Katherine Nature Preserve, Palos Heights
708-361-1873

Prairie Week
Forest Preserve District of Will County
815-727-8700

Prairie Week Celebration
Goose Lake Prairie State Natural Area, Morris
815-942-2899

October

Burgoo Festival
Downtown Utica
815-667-4861

Changing of the Leaves Festival,
Pilcher Park
815-741-7277

Fall Color Walks
Forest Preserve District of Will County
815-727-8700

Fall Colors Weekend
Starved Rock State Park
Rt. 178, Utica
815-667-4906

Halloween Spooktacular
Forest Preserve District of Will County
815-727-8700

Nature Art Fair
Little Red Schoolhouse Nature Center
Palos Preserves, Willow Springs
The Forest Preserve District of
Cook County
708-839-6897

Pioneer Crafts Festival
Pioneer Settlement, Lockport
Will County Historical Society
815-838-5080

Pumpkin Fest
Will-Joliet Bicentennial Park, Joliet
815-740-2216

Pumpkin Pie Ride (25, 50, 75, 100M)
Road and Canal Trail Rides
Peru YMCA
Starved Rock Cycling Association
815-434-7823

November

For Those Who Hunger & Thirst
5K Run/Walk, Frankfort
815-469-3750

Palos Park Turkey Trot 3M, Palos Park
708-361-1535

Pilcher Park Poultry Predictor
4M & 1M fun run, Joliet
815-478-3124

December

Camp Sagawau Cross-Country Ski Program,
Lemont
The Forest Preserve District of Cook County
630-257-2045

Winter Feeding is for the Birds
Forest Preserve District of Will County
815-727-8700

Organizations

Bicycle Clubs

Chicagoland Bicycle Federation
417 S. Dearborn, Suite 1000
Chicago, IL 60605
312-42-PEDAL

Folks on Spokes
P. O. Box 824
Homewood, IL 60430
708-730-5179

Joliet Bicycle Club
P. O. Box 2758
Joliet, IL 60436

League of Illinois Bicyclists
417 S. Dearborn, Suite 1000
Chicago, IL 60605
708-481-3429

Recreation for Individuals
Dedicated to the
Environment (RIDE)
Suite 1700, 208 S. LaSalle Street
Chicago, IL 60604
312-853-2820

Starved Rock Cycling Association
P. O. Box 2304
Ottawa, IL 61350
815-434-7823

Trail Users Rights Foundation (TURF)
P. O. Box 403
Summit, IL 60501
847-470-4266

Environmental

Friends of the Chicago River
407 S. Dearborn Suite 1580
Chicago, IL 60605
312-939-0490

Friends of the I & M Canal National
Heritage Corridor
19W580 83rd Street
Downers Grove, IL 60516
630-985-3895

Friends of the Lake Katherine
Nature Preserve
7402 Lake Katherine Drive
Palos Heights, IL 60463
708-361-1873

Friends of Pilcher Park
227 N. Gougar
Joliet, IL 60432
815-741-7277

Goose Lake Prairie Partners
Goose Lake State Natural Area
5010 North Jugtown Road
Morris, IL 60450
815-942-2899

Illinois Ornithological Society
P. O. Box 1971
Evanston, IL, 60204
847-566-4846

Midewin Tallgrass Prairie Alliance
29040 S. Cedar Road
Manhattan, IL 60442
847-566-4846

The Nature Conservancy,
Illinois Field Office
Volunteer Stewardship Office
8 S. Michigan, Suite 900
Chicago, IL 60603
312-346-8166

Prairie People Volunteers
Forest Preserve District of Will County
20851 S. Briarwood Lane
Mokena, IL 60448
815-727-8700

Save the Prairie Society
10327 Elizabeth
Westchester, IL 60154
708-865-8736

Sierra Club-Illinois Chapter
One N. LaSalle Street, Suite 4242
Chicago, IL 60602
(Includes the Chicago, Des
Plaines/Northwest Suburban, River
Prairie, Sauk-Calumet, Valley of the
Fox and Woods & Wetlands groups)
312-251-1680

Starved Rock Historical and
Education Foundation
Box 116
Utica, IL 61373
815-667-4726

Will County Chapter
Illinois Audubon Society
P. O. Box 3261
Joliet, IL 60434
815-744-7277

Hiking and Walking

American Hiking Society
P. O. Box 20160
Washington, D.C. 20041
301-565-6704

Forest Trails Hiking Club
714 W. Waveland Avenue
Chicago, IL 60613
773-248-8091

Trails

American Discovery Trail Society
P. O. Box 20155
Washington, D.C. 20041
800-663-2387

Illinois Chapter of the
Rails-to-Trails Conservancy
319 W. Cook Street,
Springfield, IL 62704
217-789-4782

Other

Illinois Trailriders
(A statewide equestrian group)
5765 Virginia
Clarendon Hills, IL 60514
630-887-8542

The Outings Club of Chicago
Outdoors Activities
520 N. Elizabeth
Lombard, IL 60148
630-268-9478

Bibliography

Books

The Complete Guide to America's National Parks. National Park Foundation. 1992–93 Edition.

Greenways for America. Little, Charles E. Johns Hopkins University Press. 1990.

Other Publications

Origin and Evolution of Illinois Counties. Printed by authority of the State of Illinois. April, 1992.

State of The Greenways Report. Prepared by Northeastern Illinois Planning Commission and Openlands Project. July, 1994.

The Northeastern Illinois Regional Greenways Plan. Developed by the Northeastern Illinois Planning Commission and Openlands Project. May, 1993.

Trails for all Americans—The Report of the National Trails Agenda Project. Submitted by American Trails to the National Park Service. Summer, 1990.

About The Team

Author/publisher, Jim Hochgesang, and his wife, Sandy, hiking and biking enthusiasts, started a publishing company, Roots & Wings, in the spring of 1993. Since then a series of five regional hiking and biking guidebooks have been published. Our other four books cover Cook, DuPage, Kane, Lake, and McHenry Counties. Roots & Wings guidebooks can be found in over 300 Chicagoland stores.

Sheryl DeVore, who edited and added natural history information to all our guidebooks, has won many first place national and regional awards for her environment and nature writing. A volunteer for the Lake County Forest Preserves, Sheryl is also chief editor of *Meadowlark, A Journal of Illinois Birds* as well as an author of many nature-related articles in national magazines. Sheryl is an ardent birder and hiker.

Melanie Lawson is a designer living and working in the Chicago area. She is also an avid hiker and biker.

Comments from Our Customers

Your comments related to this guidebook are very much appreciated for our use in improving future issues.

_____

_____

_____

_____

We are also considering publishing other hiking/biking guide-books. Would you be interested in the following?

	Level of Interest		
	High	**Medium**	**Low**
• Hiking & Biking in Lake County, Illinois—2nd Edition	☐	☐	☐
• Hiking & Biking the Grand Illinois Trail	☐	☐	☐
• Hiking & Biking in Door County, Wisconsin	☐	☐	☐
• Hiking & Biking in Southeastern Wisconsin	☐	☐	☐

We will be happy to include you on our mailing list to announce any upcoming products.

Name _____

Address _____

City, State, Zip Code _____

Thanks for your input.

You can visit us at our website at http://nsn.nslsilus.org/lfkhome/roots

Order Form

Send _____ copy/copies of Roots & Wings Hiking & Biking guidebooks to the following address:

Name _____

Address_____

City, State, Zip Code_____

Please enclose a personal check for the total amount made payable to Roots & Wings, P.O. Box 167, Lake Forest, Illinois, 60045. Thank you for your order!

_____ books @ $12.95 = _____   *Hiking & Biking in Cook County, Illinois*

_____ books @ $11.95 = _____   *Hiking & Biking in DuPage County, Illinois*

_____ books @ $12.95 = _____   *Hiking & Biking in The Fox River Valley*

_____ books @ $12.95 = _____   *Hiking & Biking the I&M Canal National Heritage Corridor*

_____ books @ $12.95 = _____   *Hiking & Biking in Lake County, Illinois,* 2nd edition (Available 4/99)

Subtotal   = _____

Illinois Residents Add Sales Tax @ 6.5%   = _____

Shipping and Handling   = _____ $1.95 _____

Total   = _____

Also you may buy our guidebooks at bookstores, bicycle shops, nature stores, and outfitters as well as other merchants throughout Chicagoland.